"Eugenia Koukounas takes us on a spiritual journey, weaving together her studies of Kabbalah, Taiji and Medicine Wheel. She deftly navigates between the profound wisdom embodied in these paths and the humanity of her daily experiences traveling them. The reader is magically brought to an emotional release and a transcendent understanding of the mysteries of life."

—Charles Brenner, *Instructor, Nanlaoshu*

more darkness to you, and you will struggle until you learn that the only answer is becoming an even brighter light."

It took me years of reading psalms daily to figure out how this lesson works. When some issue arises, it is never solely about me or about someone else. Instead, everyone involved has been given an opportunity to become wiser and more capable. And so to this day I do my daily readings with careful attention and gratitude no matter what I am being shown, because the first principle of any spiritual path is believing that the journey makes sense. That initiating principle of faith *Ehyeh Asher Ehyeh*, reminds us to be humbly aware that "I am *that*, I am *that*, I am *that*. . . ." We are all one, all the same, floating together in one boat on the same ever-changing sea of life.

During an informal class at my new dojo where no one stands in any habitual place, I decided to try the front row because I wouldn't be stepping on anyone's toes by doing so. After working on a new Taiji form for a number of years, in addition to the more than seven intensive ones I'd put in with Roy, I wanted to see if I was no longer performing like a "bent nail," a term the dojo master had used during his lifetime to describe someone coming to his class with training in a different form. Was I, once again, an advanced student?

Just before the class was about to start, a beginner tapped me on the shoulder to ask if I would return to my customary position in the corner in order for her to watch me whenever she faced that direction. Trained by Roy for so many years to put those in need first, I complied; but I was very unhappy, because only the teacher has the final say about where students stand in a classroom—and I wanted to know whether I would be allowed to remain where I had been standing in the front row. Much to my surprise, because it'd been a while since such a thing had happened, I lost my temper with the beginner.

Instantly, I saw I was in the wrong. I knew better, certainly, than to be angry with someone who was just starting out. Though our endeavors are separated by ten years of experience, that student and I share a love of Taiji, a desire to do well in the form, and the need to find our footing. I ought, instead, to have been grateful to learn that the answer to my question—whether I was once again an advanced student—was a resounding "no." Instead of being irritated with myself for reverting to old habits, I ought to have accepted the gift I'd received: Grasping what matters in Taiji, as in life, is not about *where* one stands, but about *how*.

SETTING SUN

IN POLAND, DURING MY FIRST TRAINING in Kabbalah, we stayed in farm country at a mansion converted into a hotel three hours outside Warsaw, surrounded by hay fields and orchards. There I had a chance to see what it means to partake in our shared humanity. Before breakfast, I'd go for a run, making my way through the small town, where I passed chickens casually strolling by the side of the road, scratching the earth for their next meal; a farmer who, as he did every morning at the same time, was leading his cow along the main street to some field farther down the road; and barking dogs behind fences, making themselves known. Quite a few homes had paper angels affixed to windows, while others with roomier front yards had huge crucifixes taller than a person silently guarding the property. And there I was in spandex, running to keep fit.

One morning I ventured farther and reached the railroad track. Beyond it loomed woods with very tall trees that canopied the road leading out of town. I halted to consider whether I was brave enough to enter that gloomy darkness on my own. I did an about-face for the hotel to shower and eat before the lectures commenced.

On my way back, a farmer—a man of considerable years whom I'd barely noticed as I passed him scything hay—stood straight up, his face weathered but with a smile that reached all the way to his eyes. He hailed me with a "Good morning" in Polish. I had tried to learn simple phrases in Polish from a guide book before arriving for the training, but the strings of consonants had seemed too formidable for me to begin to utter a sound.

I smiled back, still running, and in English shouted out, "Good morning." Somehow, we seemed to have understood each other perfectly well. Puzzled at my strange behavior and clothing, he asked why I was running. Without stopping, I patted my abdomen, explaining in English that I was trying to lose weight. He burst out laughing at the absurdity of such a useless expenditure of energy, especially since I wasn't overweight to start with. Scythe still firmly in his two-handed grip, he yanked his head towards the still-to-be-cut hay that stretched out endlessly before him, and invited me to join him in his daily work. That would keep off any extra weight for sure. I joined him in laughter and waved good-bye as I kept on running.

In retrospect I'm sorry I didn't stop to try my hand at wielding a scythe. But I was in a hurry—for what I didn't know—and that farmer who had devoted his life to caring for the land, and whose days were regulated by the rising and setting of the sun, the coming and going of the seasons, certainly didn't know either.

It took me a long while to catch my breath and stop running. And if ever I need a role model for standing strong and upright, shoulders squared, feet planted on the ground with a sense of humor borne of patience that keeps everything light, that farmer, who may have seen the Germans come and had certainly witnessed the Communists go, demonstrated very well that we *are* all sitting together in one boat afloat at sea. Living well is not an individual endeavor but a collective one—soul to soul, heart to heart.

FURTHER READINGS

Andrews, T. (2009) *Animal speak: The spiritual and magical powers of creatures great and small*. Woodbury, MN: Llewellyn Publications.

Andrews, T. (2011). *Simplified Qabala magic*. (2nd ed., rev.). Woodbury, MN: Llewellyn Publications.

Bodhi, B. (1999). *The noble eightfold path: Way to the end of suffering* (2nd ed., rev.) . Kandy, Sri Lanka: Buddhist Publication Society.

Campbell, J. (2001). *Thou art that: Transforming religious metaphor*. Novota, CA: New World Library.

Case, P.F. (1990). *The tarot: A key to the wisdom of the ages*. Los Angeles, CA: Builders of the Adytum.

Cloutier, D. (1980). *Spirit spirit: Shaman songs (Versions)*. Providence, RI: Copper Beech Press.

Bardon, F. (2013). *The universal master key* (1st English ed.). Norwich, England: Faulks Books.

Balch, P.A. (2012). *Prescription for herbal healing* (2nd ed.). New York: Avery.

Bear Heart, & Larkin, M. (1996). *The wind is my mother: The life and teachings of a Native American shaman*. New York: Berkley Books.

Beinfield, H., & Korngold, E. (1991). *Between heaven and earth: A guide to Chinese medicine*. Woodbury,

MN: Llewellyn Publications.

Blavatsky, H.P. (2009). *The secret doctrine* (abridged & annotated by M. Gomes). New York: Jeremy P. Tarcher/Penguin.

Budapest, Z. (1989). *The grandmother of time: A woman's book of celebrations, spells, and sacred object for every month of the year*. New York: HarperOne.

Chia, M., & North, K.D. (2010). *Taoist shaman: Practices from the wheel of life*. Rochester, VT: Destiny Books.

Chödron, P. (1997). *When things fall apart: Heart advice for difficult times*. Boston, MA: Shambhala.

Cleary, T. (2005). *The Taoist I Ching*. Boston, MA: Shambhala.

Cunningham, S. (2016). *Cunningham's encyclopedia of magical herbs* (2nd ed.). Woodbury, MN: Llewellyn.

De Armond, D. (1975). *Raven: A collection of woodcuts*. Anchorage, AL: Alaska Northwest Publishing.

——————. (1988). *The seal oil lamp: An adaptation of an Eskimo folktale*. San Francisco, CA: Sierra Club Books for Children.

Erdoes, R., & Ortiz, A. (Eds.). (1998). *American Indian trickster tales*. New York: Penguin Books.

Eisler, R. (1995). *Sacred pleasure: Sex, myth, and the*

politics of the body. New York: HarperOne.

Farmer, S. (2006). *Animal spirit guides*. Carlsbad, CA: Hay House.

Fortune, D. (2000). *Applied magic*. Boston, MA: Weiser Books.

———. (2000). *The mystical Qabalah*. Boston, MA: Weiser Books.

———. (2003). *Moon magic*. San Francisco, CA: Weiser Books.

———. (2003). *The sea priestess*. Boston, MA: Weiser Books.

———. (2005). *Dion fortune's book of the dead*. Boston, MA: Weiser Books.

Goodman, L. (1988). *Star signs: The secret code of the universe.* London: Pan McMillan.

Hall, J. (2003). *The crystal bible: A definitive guide to crystals*. Cincinnati, OH: Walking Stick Press.

Henricks, R.G. (1989). *Lao-Tzu Te-Tao Ching: A new translation based on the recently discovered Ma-wang-tui texts*. New York: Ballantine Books.

Hoffman, D. (1987). *The herbal handbook: A user's guide to medical herbalism*. Rochester, VT: Healing Arts Press

———. (1996). *The complete illustrated holistic herbal*. Boston, MA: Element Books

Huang, A. (2000). *The numerology of the I Ching: A sourcebook of symbols, structures, and traditional wisdom*. Rochester, VT: Inner Traditions.

———. (2010). *The complete I Ching: The definitive translation*. Rochester, VT: Inner Traditions.

Jou, T.H. (2000). *The Tao of I Ching: Way to divination*. Scottsdale, AZ: Tai Chi Foundation.

Kaptchuk, T.J. (2000). *The web that has no weaver: Understanding Chinese medicine*. New York: McGraw-Hill.

Lai, T.C. (1972). *The eight immortals*. Hong Kong: Swindon Book Company.

Le Guin, U.K. (2009). *Lao Tzu: Tao te Ching: A book about the way and the power of the way*. Boston, MA: Shambhala.

Lewis, C.S. (1986). *Reflections on the Psalms*. New York: HarperOne.

Man Ho, K., & O'Brien, J. (1991). *The eight immortals of Taoism: Legends and fables of popular Taoism*. New York: Penguin/Meridian books.

Mathers, S.L.M. (2006). *The key of Solomon the king*. New York: Cosimo, Inc.

Millman, D. (1993). *The life you were born to live: A guide to finding your life purpose*. Tiburon, CA: H.J. Kramer.

Ming-Dao, D. (2006). *The living I Ching: Using ancient Chinese wisdom to shape your life*. New York: HarperOne.

Mitchell, S. (Ed.). (1998). *The enlightened heart: An anthology of sacred poetry*. New York: Harper & Row.

Monroe, A.G., & Williamson, R.A. (1987). *They dance in the sky: Native American star myths*. Boston, MA: Houghton Mifflin.

Ni, H.C. (2007). *I Ching: The book of changes and the unchanging truth*. Santa Monica, CA: Seven Star Communications.

Ody, P. (1994). *The herb society's complete medicinal herbal: A practical guide to medicinal herbs, with remedies for common ailments*. London: Dorling-Kindersley.

Perry, F. (1993). *When lightning strikes a hummingbird: The awakening of a healer*. Rochester, VT: Bear & Company.

———. (1998). *The violet forest: Shamanic journeys in the Amazon*. Rochester, VT: Bear & Company.

Pinkola Estés, C. (1992). *Women who run with the wolves: Myths and stories of the wild woman archetype*. New York: Ballantine Books.

Reid, D. (1995). *The complete book of Chinese health*

and healing. Boston, MA: Shambhala.

Reyo, Z. (1994). *Mastery: The path of inner alchemy.* London: Janus.

———. (2002). *Karma and sexuality: The transforming energies of spiritual development.* London: Ashgrove Publishing.

———. (2010). *The inner woman.* Englewood Cliffs, NJ: Full Court Press.

Rinpoche, S. (1993). *The Tibetan book of living and dying* (rev. ed). (P. Gaffney & A. Harvey, Eds.). San Francisco, Ca: HarperSanFrancisco

Sams, J. (1994), *The thirteen original clan mothers.* San Francisco, CA: HarperSanFrancisco.

Sams, J., & Carson, D. (1999). *Medicine cards.* New York: St Martin's Press.

Simmons, R., & Ahsian, N. (2007). *The book of stones: Who they are and what they teach.* Berkeley, CA: North Atlantic Books.

Sun Bear, & Waban. (1992). *The medicine wheel: Earth astrology.* New York: Simon & Schuster/Fireside.

Sun Bear, Waban Wind, & Mulligan, C. (1991). *Dancing with the wheel: The medicine wheel workbook.* New York: Simon & Schuster/Fireside.

Tachi-ren, T. (2007). *What is lightbody?* Lithia Springs, CA: World Tree Press.

Thorsson, E. (1984). *A handbook of rune magic*. San Francisco, CA: Weiser Books.

Three Initiates. (2008). *The Kybalion: A study of the Hermetic philosophy of ancient Egypt and Greece*. New York: Penguin/ Jeremy P. Tarcher.

Thurman, R.A., (1994. *The Tibetan book of the dead: Liberation through understanding in the between*. San Francisco, CA: HarperSanFrancisco.

Trungpa, C. (1999). *Great Eastern sun: The wisdom of shambala*. Boston, MA: Shambhala.

Wallis, V. (2004). *Two old women: An Alaska legend of betrayal, courage, and survival*. New York: HarperCollins/Perennial.

Wilhelm, R., & Baynes, C.F. (Trans.). (1997). *The I Ching or book of changes*. Princeton, NJ: Princeton University Press.

Wang, R. (1987). *Qabalistic tarot: A textbook of mystical philosophy*. York Beach, ME: Samuel Weiser.

Wong, E. (1990). *Seven taoist masters: A folk novel of China*. Boston, MA: Shambhala.

———. (2001). *Tales of the taoist immortals*. Boston, MA: Shambhala.

ABOUT THE AUTHOR

Eugenia Koukounas has degrees in both politics and nursing, has had a background in journalism, and writes both nonfiction and fiction. She has studied and practiced Taiji for twelve years, and Kaballah and Shamanism for thirteen. She is currently at work on a modern tea-cozy entitled *Winslow's Promise*. She lives with her husband, the novelist and poet Barry Sheinkopf, in Northern New Jersey.

www.ingramcontent.com/pod-product-compliance
Lightning Source LLC
Chambersburg PA
CBHW051650040426
42446CB00009B/1073

ALL OUR RELATIONS

ALL OUR RELATIONS
One Path to Devotional Practice

Eugenia Koukounas

With a Foreword by Foster John Perry

Full Court Press
Englewood Cliffs, New Jersey

First Edition

Copyright © 2017 by Eugenia Koukounas

All rights reserved. No part of this book may be reproduced or transmitted in any form or by any means electronic or mechanical, including by photocopying, by recording, or by any information storage and retrieval system, without the express permission of the author, except where permitted by law.

Published in the United States of America
by Full Court Press, 601 Palisade Avenue,
Englewood Cliffs, NJ 07632
fullcourtpressnj.com

Reach Eugenia Koukounas at ekoukounas@hotmail.com

ISBN 978-1-938812-96-5
Library of Congress Catalog No. 2017944464

*Editing and book design by Barry Sheinkopf
for Bookshapers (bookshapers.com)*

Cover art, "Street, Truchas, NM," by Barry Sheinkopf

Taiji symbol courtesy istockphoto.com

*Graphic rendering of the author's Medicine Wheel
by Richard Donatone*

*All other art by Roy Lucianna,
courtesy Estate of Roy Lucianna*

To my husband
who listened even when he didn't believe
and
To my mother, Aspasia Koukounas
who urged me to write this book

Acknowledgments

I want to thank Barry Sheinkopf, who has had the difficult job of wearing many hats in helping to bring this book to fruition—teacher, editor, book designer, and husband. He has juggled them all with grace, patience, wit, and wisdom. This book would never have happened without his love and support.

I am grateful to Foster John Perry and Kristos Tsompanclis Perry for never giving up on me, for lovingly shoving me out of the nest in spite of my reluctance when it was time to move on, and for writing the foreword.

My thanks to Jane Gardner, whose tireless effort pushed me to make this book as clear as possible; and also to Susan Balaban, who knows me better than I do and helped me see what I had to offer.

My thanks to Karen Nickeson, Richard Donatone, and Gail Ryan for their friendship, generosity, and support. I am most appreciative to Richard for reading the book and for the graphic rendering of my medicine wheel.

My thanks to my brother Michael, a polite skeptic in esoteric matters who insisted on reading the manuscript and asked questions that I hadn't thought to ask.

I am thankful to Charles Brenner, my Taiji teacher at Nanlaoshu, for his patience and guidance, and to

Shu Ching Shih, a powerhouse of a writer, who told me, when I was making no progress, "To write a book you need to be disciplined, but to finish a book you need to be selfish."

My thanks to Arlene and Howard Pollack, Leigh Reznik, Maria Santoro, Carmen Young, Aysegul Sevil, and Janice Kochanski, who read portions of the manuscript and gave me their feedback and encouragement.

I am grateful to Zulma Reyo, whose love and support I've always felt—especially when teaching me how to cut through self-pity.

I want to thank Agostino Di Bari for his thoughtful support.

My thanks to Robert Lavett Smith, and to fellow members of the Wednesday Evening seminar at Writing Center as well—Edmund Dollinger, Rita Kornfeld, Natalie Beaumont, Adele Schwartz, Harold Steinbach, Ora Melamed, Tony Wiersielis, Gail Larkin, Bill Paladino, Carl Schell, and the late Peter Levy (who once pulled me aside and whispered out of Barry's hearing, "If you want to write about angels, go ahead and *do* it"). Their help has been invaluable, because they questioned anything that wasn't absolutely clear to them.

And finally, my gratitude to Roy Lucianna for his willingness to take me on.

—E.K.

August 2017

> (Any brute
> can buy a machine in a shop,
> but the sacred spells are secret to the kind,
> and if power is what we wish
> they won't work.)
>
> —*W. H. Auden,*
> *"The Common Life"*

FOREWORD

As a Shaman, the life of our spirit is to explore, to travel, and experience the core of ourselves, and to know ourselves in the mirror of our Creator. We choose to fathom the compassion and majesty of the consciousness of the universe. When Earth was created like a jewel in the cosmos, we made a choice to come here, arriving as spirits on Earth, fashioning our own bodies through the Five Elements intimately. Our spirits entered stones and their consciousness of timelessness. The Stone people, as we call them, remain immortal, as witnesses to vast moments of time, like meteors journeying through space, adding their qualities to each world they touch. The Stones taught us how to remain immortal in the depth of meditation, to become witnesses to the ecstasy of Creation. We had entered a new unique world of Nature.

We entered as spirits into the Tree people to explore the Dryads, the spirit of trees—to remain optimistic, joyful, in the contentment and peace of trees and their forest of antennas. We learned the language of trees to live on Earth and thrive. We learned to grow tall, upright, with dignity and grace. We became the trees. We descended into animals, creating chimeras—half human, half animal creations. We immersed ourselves in the attributes of each animal, depending on and incorporating their keen instincts. We became the deer, the ox, the bear, the turtle, the whale, and the eagle; and their inspiration allowed us to live on Earth in harmony with Nature. We became all animals to learn how to live on Earth, to desire life in all its diversity, forming a kinship with a new world of senses The breath became our moment of creation at birth, linking our bodies to greater cycles of the cosmos. Our blood became our signature, linking us to the oceans. We became the soil, linking the stars to the minerals of Earth to fashion our bodies from seed, from corn, through the plants, illuminated by the sun and reflected in the moon. We were becoming highly evolved plants in the garden.

We descended like hermaphrodites into bodies that now embodied all of Nature, slowly distinguishing light and shadow, male and female within ourselves—a wholeness and a plurality. We entered an evolution that encompassed all of Earth's creatures, and we embodied all that we learned as spirits in our descent into form, as sparks of the fire of our Creator formed in our hearts, and inspiration molded our intelligence.

We created a purpose out of choice; we created our own meaning to become meaning makers. Our thoughts became living things that also wanted form. Our will, aligned with Nature, sought harmony, development, and to go beyond ourselves—as above, so below and beyond. We created rhythms to sustain our thoughts as disciplines. We felt our soul in matter, and we felt our own creation through all the spirits of Nature in our bodies. We felt a new existence, a new consciousness, that was changing matter through feeling thoughts. As we imbued thoughts with greater feeling, our thought forms began to have a life of their own—becoming independent of us. We had to learn self-control, to master ourselves, to choose our thoughts and witness the repercussions of our own actions.

Our great fall was to separate from the Nature we were born through. When we began to look down on Nature, to judge on our own creations, we began the unhappiness of shame and guilt that separates the core of our soul from our created life. When we no longer listened to the core purpose we had created to explore here, we left our own selves and became detached from our bodies. We began to listen to others, to their opinions, and chose to listen to others above ourselves, leading to the many separations that have resulted in our current anxiety and malaise. This created untold manipulations from outside ourselves—seeking our attention, as thought forms grew into unsustainable habits and manipulated religions. We had separated so far from our unique nature, our core, and had forgotten the essence of our creation and our self-created purpose.

Shamans learned to remember. To remember we had to remember our creation, the will to know, to become infinite. Knowledge, love, trust began as we entered the archives, the morphogenetic library of this world and the worlds we came from. As we attuned ourselves back to the rhythms of our own heartbeat, and aligned our bodies to the spirits of Nature, we learned how we shared this world with many other life forms, seen and unseen. We developed our awareness to take in the cornucopia of existences here and learn through them. Shamans learned from angels, who instructed them how to transcend themselves.

To master ourselves, we needed examples—as in Kabbalah; we looked to people like Enoch, who invited the angels to teach himself how to follow himself. Through the alchemy of plant, tree, animal, and the elemental teachings, he went beyond himself through the power of his belief. Through this strong belief, a determined will, and by choosing his mission, he became an archangel. Unlike all other archangels, he was human and therefore had gone beyond the angels who protected his development. These masters, and there are many, left their footprints on Earth for us to follow. They left their achievements and the pathways of attainment. The angels gave us the Kabbalah, the Tree of Life, its many doors, the pathways of the thirty-two ways to development as a soul in a body. Most of all, we learned that we must master our breath to master air, master our blood through frequencies of sound to change our DNA though attunement, and master our thought forms out of negative habits to realize that once we give in to thought forms that constantly need to be fed, paid attention to, and can eventually create a world of illusion around us. Once we face what we create, take responsibility for our creations, and release the manipulations in this world and their influence on us, we become free.

Self-control is freedom. Conscious direction of our thoughts, trusting our feeling, is the return to nature—to follow our own paths, to complete our time in this world and journey onward beyond time like the stones, to explore inner and outer space. The angels—the Thrones, the Principalities, protected our development, to go beyond ourselves. When we remember our core nature, our chosen purpose, and give voice and action to it, we climb the mountain to heal our ancestors, our past lives, and our childhood. Enoch achieved all this in order to become his final attainment—Urgaya, the greatest achievement as a human being. We now climb that mountain, like hermits, in a solitary climb that eventually all of humanity must make. Become a pathway for others to follow. No matter what happens in the evolution of Earth, there are parallel realities to continue our progress into self-realization. The snows on the mountain peaks are mirrors, reflecting back thought to the spirit of the mountain.

To pass to the level of Enoch individually, we must know what surrounds the mountain top—the twelve goddesses, the women who circle this attainment and who attained this self-mastery, like Isis, Diana, Hekate, and their many other names in diverse cultures. They are the queens who surround those who remember and master their body and mind. Beneath these women are the twenty-two masters who ascended and managed, through feeling and discipline, to remain in their core nature connected to all of life. They are immortals who embraced their bodies, and descended with their core self to transform—by choice, by belief, and through repeated actions and movement—a mastery of life. This result is the light that every Shaman follows, and every Kabbalist knows, as we embrace the physical totally and embrace nature to attain real wholeness and the depth of magic.

This pathway of thirty-two steps in Kabbalah, lived by Taoist immortals and many great Shamans who have found the power within, is outlined beautifully by Eugenia Koukounas, who has lived her life by following her core self back to her original soul. She teaches you to become original, to climb the mountain of how we were created, to pass like Enoch through self-mastery, to become the archangel Metatron, and finally to transcend himself as Urgaya—the human, archangelic, and mastered self. Like Buddha, Christ, the prophets, and the enlightened Shamans and healers, we have a clear path to free ourselves from all manipulations created over time. We embrace our alignment back to water, air, fire, earth, and akasha. We, like our guide in this book, Eugenia, can first heal ourselves, to carry our own light as hermits, with the lamp in front of us, on the top of our chosen mountain, for others to follow us out of the darkness. Follow your own light, as we are never alone in this journey, and step by step, through practice, we breathe like mountains.

—*Foster John Perry*
Mt. Shasta,
August 6, 2017

TABLE OF CONTENTS

A Doorway to Freedom, *1*
Crown, *13*
Rising Sun, *21*
Between Heaven and Earth, *27*
Wisdom, *39*
Understanding, *45*
Mercy, *53*
Strength, *59*
Midday Sun, *65*
Stillness, *73*
Midnight Sun, *83*
Beauty, *95*
Victory, *103*
Glory, *111*
Foundation, *119*
Kingdom, *127*
Setting Sun, *133*

Further Readings, 141

A DOORWAY TO FREEDOM

> *"I could say 'Elves' to him,*
> *But it's not elves exactly, and I'd rather*
> *He said it for himself."*
>
> —Robert Frost

THIS BOOK IS NOT ABOUT the disappointments I've lived through. I now see them as gifts that propelled me to take refuge in Taiji, Kabbalah, and the Medicine Wheel, where I eventually discovered that the issues that once weighed heavily on me mattered very little. I have let go of the past and remain in the present now.

This book is, instead, about how I came to grips with anger, pride, a judgmental nature, and impatience, to name but a few of the obstacles that I've had to overcome in the journey to devotion. As a result, I have no one left to blame, not even myself, for the life I'm leading. It didn't happen overnight, which is why the chapters in the book often echo each other. But it didn't take me long to comprehend the joy and freedom I've gained from doing this work.

But that's me. You may very well ask how any of this can possibly matter to you. Here's how.

I doubt you live a monastic life. If you're like me and most other people I know, you're up to your elbows in the daily grind, multi-tasking your way through check-off lists. You juggle home, work, and family, see friends, and do a hundred other things. Over time and without notice, the anxiety produced in meeting one deadline after another erodes your health and ends in an exhaustion—physical, but emotional and spiritual as well—that's not easy to recover from.

When, and more importantly *how*, do you ever have time to put what is crucial to you into perspective and not withdraw completely from the world? Are *you* able to sit still for even ten minutes without reaching for some distraction, electronic or otherwise? Pascal rightly said, "All of humanity's problems stem from man's inability to sit quietly in a room alone."

All Our Relations describes how I have reached equilibrium through daily practice, learned to stand on my own two feet, and become joyful, optimistic, and creative. At its core, the book is not about a *particular* spiritual path taken in life, but about the spirit in which *any* path is taken. It shows the intention needed to travel a road of your own choosing.

EACH OF THE SIXTEEN CHAPTERS to follow considers a particular aspect of the Kabbalistic Tree of Life or the Native American Medicine Wheel, or demonstrates Taoist theory through my endeavor to learn Taiji.

What are these three disciplines? In brief (because it would take an entire book to explain the complexities of each), Taiji-chuan, the complete name for Taiji, literally means "supreme ultimate fist." There is no agreement about when Taiji originated in China, but it started as a martial art that was later modified into a means of achieving harmony of mind and body to promote health and longevity. Kabbalah, which means "to receive," is an ancient Jewish mystical tradition, of which I practice a modified version, that aims to reveal the relationship between the Divine and oneself in order to achieve self-mastery. The Medicine Wheel, in its simplest form, is physically a circle of stones with a single stone in the center that maps out the four cardinal directions of the Earth and the transitions that take place among them. Walking the Wheel, which requires more than simply walking, is a way of achieving harmony with Nature and is, like the other two disciplines, a tool to bring you to a balanced, centered self.

I've tried to show that, while they have not blended together, these three disciplines are so intricately entwined for me that each is able to shed clarity on the others.

I know that the Medicine Wheel, Taiji, and Kabbalah can each be studied for decades before understanding sinks deeply enough into a person's essence to become one with their breath. But I cannot look at a flower without its shape expressing some unfolding movement in the Taiji form, or reflect on the brevity of its existence without recalling the brevity of all life alluded to more than once in the Psalms of the Old Testament. Nor do I forget that the flower's sheer beauty is medicine for body and soul.

And though the stories I tell are meant to illustrate concepts I've set forth at the beginning of each chapter, these tales share the fundamental principle of diligence as a way of coming to devotion, and coming closer to one's personal definition of the Divine. This book is about how I chose to pursue my spiritual work on a daily basis even when nothing happened for long stretches of time, when I was frustrated, tired, scattered, or rushed, and even more when I failed to preserve my spiritual equilibrium. I just kept going. I do so to this day.

A DOORWAY TO FREEDOM

IN ESOTERIC WORK, with so many paths to choose from that are readily available, it's easy to get distracted and go from one thing to another, seeking an encounter that replicates the euphoria one experienced in some previous lecture, workshop, or healing. Walking down any new spiritual path, however, is like embarking on a new romance—it's all amazing stuff, but in esoteric work, just as in a budding love affair, someone eventually has to take out the garbage. That small necessity can test the romance right out of a relationship, just as getting down to the business of taking a good long look at yourself, and applying the tools available, can strain the initial joy of meeting a truly life-changing teacher.

How one expresses devotion is a very personal matter. There are as many roads to it as there are that lead to Rome. Some do it fly-fishing or through the arts, still others through caring for loved ones or making it a point, day by day, to be patient or just. Whatever the choice, when done with awareness, the expression propels us beyond the limits of our five senses and daily needs, so that we do not simply live like grass—sprouting, growing, aging, and dying. Instead, our focused attempts increase our awareness of spirit, which diminishes the divide between ourselves and others.

When I began this endeavor in Kabbalah, I chose to

work through the Tree of Life. Comprised of ten spheres that reflect different aspects of our souls, they aren't ac-

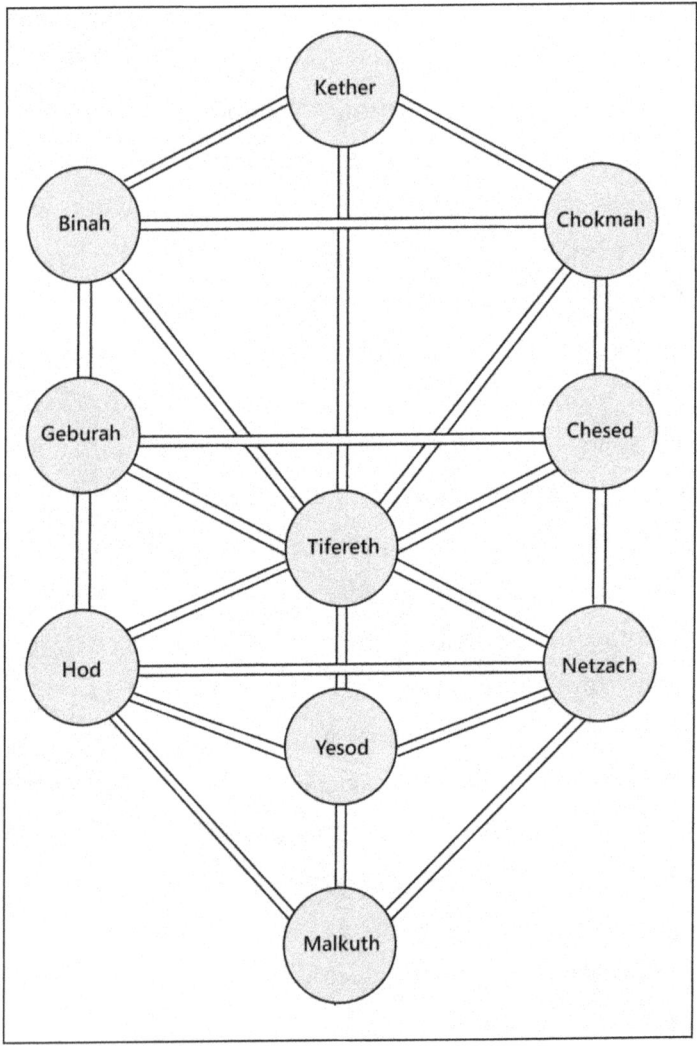

The Tree of Life

tually segmented *parts* of each of us. They do, however, offer a useful schematic to reflect upon how to get past habitual blocks.

For predetermined periods of time, I tackled an overall theme—such as mercy, strength, or wisdom—and measured myself against it. In addition, I read the psalms, each of which has a quality one can focus on to make a shift and, by reading them, get help in some way or another just for the asking.

Each morning I said prayers to highlight what I wanted to change based on the theme of the sphere I was immersed in. At first, what I chose to work on—and how—depended on where I thought I was falling short in personal integrity. Eventually, I got to the root of my limited capacity for, say, forgiveness and figured out what I needed to do to overcome my resistances. I learned, first, to focus, then to be patient, and finally to slow down enough to be able to listen to my soul, which in turn helped me to become accountable for my behavior. In time, that helped me to be kind to myself in order—just as importantly—to be kind to others.

My prayers were always answered, though *not* always in the ways I had hoped. Certain themes came up regularly, and I worked through them in meditation, making adjustments to my behavior, thoughts, and emotions till I got them right—at least right for that moment. In time, I changed enough to begin to feel gratitude, not for what I had gained or even what I hoped to gain, but for the privilege of being on the journey at all.

I HAD FIRST TAKEN UP the challenge of Taiji, in tandem with Kabbalah, to learn patience. An experienced paramedic once told me that she had tried Taiji, but that it hadn't seemed to work for her. I sympathized completely and explained that Taiji is not for the faint of heart.

Taiji Symbol

There are—in my form, at least—108 steps to memorize in sequence, but resistance to learning any move is experienced, not only on a physical level, but emotionally, mentally, and spiritually as well. It takes practice to smooth out the jagged edges in your body movement, as well as your life, once you take all these levels into account.

She immediately got it, pointing out that, after many years of observation, she knew who was more likely to heal successfully: They were the ones who engaged in making positive shifts from within and were willing to ask for help to make those necessary changes.

Along with patience, Taiji also became a vehicle for physical, then emotional, balance. Doing the form fills me with peace and joy. It reinforced the same principles I was trying to learn through Kabbalah. Practice has helped regulate my breath, mind, and movement. It has stripped away an overzealous desire to strive for excellence. I have realized instead that this pursuit has its own rhythm, and that nothing I do can hurry that along. In fact, any attempt to interfere with it usually means an unexpected setback.

No matter how beautifully one manages to execute a move in Taiji, it is never scraped down to its true essence if one has not tamed anger, impatience, and pride. Without reaching a sense of stillness, the form remains elusive. All its moves, from initiation to completion, express an arc of *yin* and *yang*, an ebbing and flowing energy that is represented by the Taiji symbol, which illustrates a never-ending flow from the one state to the other.

To be truly empty in Western culture is not easy, though without letting go completely in a Taiji move the reverse is equally impossible—to be fully animated in it. It's only when I let whatever is happening simply happen, free of any personal agenda, that I do better in the form.

THE MEDICINE WHEEL is an internal clock that measures the calendar year, our lives, and our hopes and dreams, reminding us that change is the only constant in life. The Wheel showed me how to embrace change by deepening my understanding that there is a season for everything. This in turn has helped me to know where I am standing at any given moment, and to see what is presently happening around me from a long-term perspective.

Walking the Wheel has heightened my thankfulness for being alive by connecting me to the many faces of Nature. I cannot look at the world without acknowledging that all living beings are interconnected, and that even what we consider inanimate is alive, like the stones at our

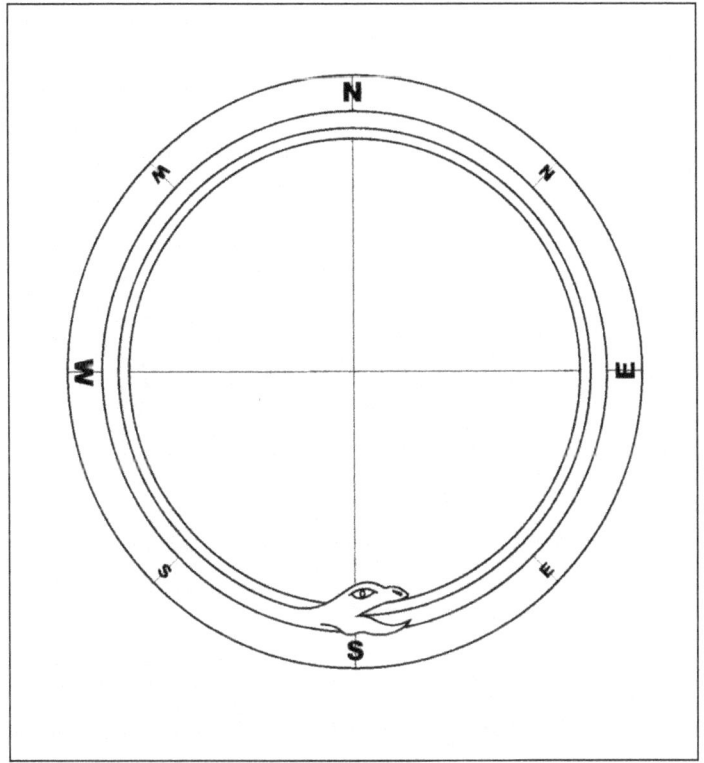

An example of a Medicine Wheel

feet. Through the Wheel I've come to understand how the four elements—air, fire, water, and earth—permeate our lives, and have found solace as well as wisdom in how Nature works.

All of this has taken me down a road that keeps opening up in surprising ways and remains a joy and a challenge—and I wouldn't want it any other way. As you read about it, remember what I've done is not what I suggest you do. The important thing is *how* I've done it. You find your way.

CROWN

KETHER, WHICH MEANS "CROWN" in Hebrew, is the first of ten spheres on the Tree of Life, closest to Divinity, reflecting its brilliant light. It's the spark that initiates you into the Tree of Life and its descent down the other nine spheres. It is the transition point into spiritual growth, where souls either leave Divinity to enter individuality (a life), or depart in the reverse direction to return to Divinity (a death). In other words, we come into this life through Kether and leave it the same way. Traveling up and down the Tree is the work of a lifetime, a personal effort to monitor and adjust from within whatever you need, in order to live joyously and productively.

But that initiating spark is really love of the Divine—what we can call faith, our personal covenant, which we have endless opportunity in our daily lives to express.

Whether you're having a good or bad day, losing or gaining faith at any given moment, wandering as the Jews wandered in the desert for forty years—basically an adult's lifetime of effort—Kether represents the first step in deepening personal faith and, ultimately, building the integrity that goes with it. Allow Kether's initiation of faith to flow into your endeavors, and before you know it, in the blink of an eye or a lifetime, you've arrived where you need to be.

The ups and downs of life are also expressed in the Taiji symbol. It consists of two mirrored images—*yang*, a field of white that represents hot, bright, high, dry, boisterous, and masculine, to list but a few descriptions, and that contains a black dot; and the opposite, *yin*, a black field that represents cold, dark, low, wet, quiet, and feminine, and contains a white dot. When, for instance, summer (or joy) is in full force, shown by the thickest portion of white in the symbol, very little, if any, of the black is to be seen along its side. It is all one continuous flow with each experience equally important, so that how many dark or bright days we've gathered in a lifetime is not really the point. Experiencing dark and light fully, knowing that, for every moment of light, there's of necessity an equivalent moment of darkness waiting to take place at some other random moment (and vice versa), we eventually learn how our life force works in its entirety. In order to execute the Taiji form, or a life, well, we must therefore be capable of yielding as well as doing. It is, of course, true that what we put into a life is what we get out. But fully comprehending the *rhythms* of it eventually allows us to gain something even greater in return. It's one way to make sense of what the Whirlwind meant when demanding of Job, "Where wast thou when I laid the foundations of the Earth?"

Nurturing personal integrity has been a challenge for me, because I've had to learn to keep in check a tendency to want to be noticed for the efforts I've made. The hunger for praise has resulted in many unhappy choices. But as I've learned to curb this unfortunate trait—it always remains a conscious choice—and instead exercised my personal definition of integrity, I sleep better at night. Otherwise, when I doubt myself or my choices, when I feel as if what I do doesn't amount to much or matter in the slightest, or, worse, when I feel put out because it hasn't been noticed and therefore hasn't turned out the way I expected, I can become almost paralyzed by despondency.

Eventually, though, I pull myself together, quite often by keeping in mind what St. Francis said: "All the darkness in the world cannot extinguish the light of a single candle." Remembering to look for the light or, even better becoming the light, has been my personal goal in traversing the Tree of Life.

In my love-hate relationship with prepping the Taiji classroom for a number of years in a haunted church, there came a period when I chose to read individual psalms to address the needs of each member of the class. I didn't think much about the act other than that I loved the psalms, and that doing so gave me a chance to read more of them. It seemed to me a sensible thing to do. For weeks on end, I'd consider what psalm each person needed at that moment and read it for them. One evening, instead of opening my Bible to the Psalms, I accidentally opened to something else, which I no longer recall. My eyes fell on a verse that, in effect, said I have taken care of sacred spaces for generations and have been blessed for doing so.

Something was letting me know that my work had indeed been noticed, even if the beneficiaries were not consciously aware of what I was doing on their behalf. I was astonished by the acknowledgment, having not asked for it, but like a candle glowing in darkness, I was being reminded that I needn't see the outcome, only keep faith.

But having faith isn't fixed in place like some painting hung on a wall. In very human terms, faith falters, swells, and falters only to swell again, like the Taiji symbol, because the forces at work are attempting to maintain a balance. The symbol, like life, is always moving. So even though I loved the psalms and the prayers that I recited daily, I would on occasion have my doubts.

One evening as I finished setting up the classroom physically as well as energetically with a Native American invocation to the four directions—calling in the spirit animals dedicated to East, West, North, and South—I wondered about those animals. After years of uttering the words in daily prayers, and twice a week in preparation for class, I questioned whether the serpent from the South, the jaguar from the West, the hummingbird from the North, and the eagle from the East actually entered the room when I called them, and if they did, whether I'd be able to see them.

When the seated meditation began that night in class, I chose a direction that I didn't usually take—with my back to the West. As I closed my eyes and tried to clear my mind, I became aware of a presence behind me, a coiling energy that was about to spring forward, and I briefly imagined a perfectly poised black jaguar ready to pounce. *Okay*, I said to myself, as I usually do in such a situation, *you are imagining things*, and tried to ignore that tremendous force behind me. But in response to my doubt, it drew nearer and brought its muzzle to my ear. It was dead winter; no heating vent or breeze from a leaky window could possibly have resembled the warm breath of something alive directed into my right ear. Sufficiently chastised, I sighed and silently told it, *Okay, I will never doubt you again.* The cat backed away and melted into nothingness, and I was left with a humbling certainty that, at the very least, repetition of prayer brings results.

While I have contemplated Kether on any number of occasions, it was only after I gave it my attention for a full twelve months, part of a ten-year endeavor dedicating one year to each sphere of the Tree of Life, that I began to get a glimmer of understanding. Just before I started, Kristos Tsompanelis, who taught me Kabbalah, gave me a magic formula, a prayer—Kabs am pekht (light in expansion), knox om pax (connected in peace)—that I've uttered every day since, in the hope that my daily behavior might eventually match this prayer. Somewhat daunted by the task of approaching the unknowable Kether only as a perpetual novice, I flailed about over how to undergo that year of study.

I recalled how Kristos had once explained that Kether can be seen as the answer God gave Moses when Moses asked for God's name: "*Ehyeh asher ehyeh,*" which literally translates as "I am that I am," but which Kristos takes as, "I am *that*, I am *that*, I am *that*," meaning that God is present in all things.

So I surrendered myself to the vastness of Kether by naming the Divine in 108 different ways to stress just that principle. Clear quartz is one of the stones that can represent Kether; I made a *mala* (a Hindu rosary) of 108 beads of clear quartz. In the morning I lit a candle, a six-by-three-inch pillar of white beeswax, and sat cross-legged on my bed to do my meditation, which consisted of uttering, in Hebrew, 108 versions of the Name of God as I counted out each bead.

As I sang out the first of the names—I'd chosen *Ehyeh Asher Ehyeh* to lead the list—my beloved cat, Seenee, who for years would burrow deeper into my side, happily dozing through all my meditations and psalm readings, suddenly picked up her head, gave me a baleful look for inviting such intense energy into *her* space, jumped off the bed, and departed without a glance back. Left alone to face a challenging expenditure of energy, after chanting the first few names, I felt an intense column of light, not unlike some sci-fi laser beam, pour over me, burning away bits and pieces of everyday life that were not in tune with that brilliance. I'd finish somewhat overwhelmed but lighter and ready to meet the day.

Entering Kether requires the fearlessness to go beyond doubt, beyond embarrassment and hedging one's bets, to free-fall into a vast, incomprehensible light (in both going towards death or coming to life), and to face the overwhelming possibility that I, too, am *that*, and I am *that*, and I am *that*, because I share space, love, energy, and purpose with all things on this Earth.

In other words, to me Kether means what I have recited daily in my Native American prayer: That I am grateful to be at one with all my relations—the stone people, the plant people, the four-legged, the two-legged, the creepy-crawlers, the finned, the furred, and the winged ones, living this song of life. I consciously choose to share with them my efforts to surrender to divine brilliance, which requires, at the very least, diligence, and, with any luck, a deep faith to find my way.

RISING SUN

East on the Medicine Wheel represents illumination, dawn, spring, childhood—the eagle soaring towards Heaven, looking ahead to the future. And like Kether, which initiates you into the Tree of Life, East initiates you into new beginnings: life unfolding with limitless possibilities and steeped in hope. While we are young, we have the luxurious sense that we have all the time in the world to let those hopes unfold.

First light brings a fresh perspective on the world around us, gained by that very light, which can naturally influence our mindset mostly for the better. Wisdom is achieved precisely by expanding our viewpoint, like an eagle's; it's impossible, seeing a bigger picture to remain small-minded or wholly earthbound by our daily worries.

Dawn challenges me. Not always a good sleeper, I

sometimes struggle to get up and do so animated only by a desire to be with my husband, who awakens before first light twice a week to teach an eight o'clock class. I stumble out of bed. As I reach for the coffee pot and fill it with water, many times without thinking, I start offering makeshift thanks for water being readily available, clean, and safe. Whatever water I don't use for coffee goes to water the plants in the living room as I stare at the apartment buildings across the street. I rarely see another light on. I give thanks for having a home, for being healthy and strong, for being blessed to have my family and my friends—for having this life, and the joy of this moment, regardless of the challenges I may be facing. I'm always especially grateful for the gift of conversing with my husband over breakfast, sharing insights that are keenest in the early morning, unhampered by fatigue that creeps in as the day goes by.

When he leaves, before I clear away the breakfast dishes and make the bed to establish a calm and serene living space for prayer, I spend some time at the table, letting my mind wander, lucky if I happen upon some insight that may be of use to me.

I begin the process of meditation by lighting a candle, creating my own "first" light, and by burning incense, allowing my prayers to rise along with the smoke. I'm happy it's still very early in the day because I can leave the everyday world behind for a bit longer.

At times, my schedule prevents early morning meditation, and though I will find time to pray later in the day, it doesn't feel the same once the hustle-and-bustle overtakes the fragile quiet. No matter how hard I try later on to capture the essence of morning prayer, it's never as deep or as still, and I am not quite as grounded as I need to be for whatever life throws my way.

I speak of prayer here as if the meaning of the word is clear. But that may not be the case. Sometimes, as I have just suggested, prayer is a way of saying thanks. But it has other functions as well, including shifting us mentally and emotionally for the better. This respite from the usual din in our lives allows the opportunity, not only to express a desire for something better, but to see our way clear to achieving it.

An old friend, whose own studies have taken her on a path parallel to mine, once startled me by saying, "You know, you are practically dripping with devotion."

Well. . . maybe, I thought, always ready to list whatever issues I still need to work on or *have* worked on but require continued vigilance with, because we are all more human than not. Habit is hard to break. Still, I found her choice of words interesting because I have visualized my daily psalm work like drops of water landing in an empty bucket. I am very committed to this building effort.

I was taught, Kabbalistically speaking, that each of the first seventy-two psalms, written by King David, has the power to move a particular challenge at its core for the better. Reading a psalm with devotion eventually works, though it may not provide the result you have in mind. No matter how many ups and downs I have experienced, my hope has remained that, eventually, enough drops will have accumulated in that bucket for me to make significant shifts.

Indeed, I've developed a conversation of sorts with the psalms. Instead of driving myself crazy about one issue or another that I think I need to deal with, before opening the Bible I ask the question, *What do I need to know today?* and add *Thank you for your guidance.* When I open up the Bible, the psalm that my eyes fall upon may sometimes be a surprise, but it is never off the mark.

As I've grown more familiar with the psalms—interestingly, the same five or ten usually come up over a period of weeks while I'm addressing some issue in my life—I can over time drill down and explore them with an expanded insight. Whether the message is to let me know that I've screwed up, am too hard on myself or not hard enough, need to clean up my act or let go of a situation, or be reminded that someone has my back and not to worry so much—the psalms show me that there is always another way to look at my current situation.

For example, when I ask, What do I need to know today? and get Psalm 37, which is the psalm to soothe and quiet one's nerves and overcome jealousy, for years I thought it meant for me that I had to look for jealousy in myself. While not pleasant to admit it to oneself, it is necessary to face envying another person in order to make a break with that emotion's life-negating force.

As I trained myself to eliminate the habit of comparing myself to anyone else, and instead to accept myself for who and what I am, there came a point that when I got Psalm 37 and I could honestly scan myself to find nothing. And I began to consider the possibility that the psalm might be pointing to someone else's jealousy. This used to send me into a frenzy of wondering who, what, when, where, and why. But these questions, too, in the end became insignificant to me as I delved further into my morning devotions. Once I quelled my outrage *and* my curiosity, the answer to those questions didn't matter at all.

Nowadays, whether I can identify jealousy in me or

in another person is immaterial to the situation. I have reached a more encompassing view and realized that, by focusing instead on soothing my nerves, I become prepared for whatever will come my way. Whether, in a moment of weakness, someone else will be jealous of me, or I of them, the only answer to the dilemma is for me to calm down for my own sake as well as theirs. This shift is a direct result of these extended acts of devotion—my personal work in the morning light giving me the expanded sight gained from an eagle's perspective.

BETWEEN HEAVEN AND EARTH

SUNLIGHT, STARLIGHT, AND CANDLELIGHT are all metaphors for a flame that opens the heart to express love. During one of those serious Nor-Easters that occasionally hit and disable the New York Metropolitan Area, my husband and I lost our electricity, hot water, and heat. We were among the lucky ones; our power was out for a mere twenty-six hours.

As darkness fell and the storm moved on, we were about to climb seven flights of stairs to reach our apartment when he asked, "What am I going to do with no power?"

"What you always do," I answered. "Read. But this time the way they did more than a hundred years ago—by candlelight."

While my search to shorten the distance between the

Divine and me as much as is humanly possible has often led me down a road with no particular destination in mind, one usually needs some kind of illumination when looking for something. This has left me with a lot of candles that I use in these many acts of devotion—handmade beeswax candles to read psalms by; pink, brown, white, blue, and red candles, each serving a specific prayer to a particular end.

A supply of small white paraffin candles are also part of my cache, which I once used to encircle the members of the Taiji class, protecting us from ghosts that inhabited the church where we met. We had realized that we could no longer explain away the rattling about in the room, the opening doors, and heavy footsteps that shuffled into our space while we silently meditated or did the form. Or when we heard someone playing a piano in a hallway although everyone in the building was accounted for in the classroom, or when there were only three of us in the entire building, yet as we sat in lotus position chanting, "Om," we eerily heard a fourth voice, female, coming from within the room, chanting along with us.

I have had two people of Chinese descent explain in a matter-of-fact way what was going on. The woman said that, in her culture, if her car broke down at night between a temple and a cemetery, and she had to sleep in one place or the other, she'd choose the cemetery, because all the ghosts would be attracted to the light of the temple. The man, on hearing the goings-on at the church during our Taiji class, shrugged and explained, "If you do Taiji and are beyond a beginner's level, you become a light, and ghosts are attracted to you."

This second explanation hit home, particularly because my personal experience of our form very much felt to me as if I were expressing a physical prayer. So the image of becoming a light drawing in lost souls was not so far fetched, especially since our teacher, Roy Lucianna, would, on occasion, assure us that the gods were pleased whenever we do the form. Once I fully understood what was going on, when he repeated that little nugget, I'd mumble under my breath, "Them and a whole lot of others."

Out of a sense of duty to help, since I *am* a driven Virgo, when the whole room went 1960s horror movie one night with smoky air billowing in the room while the proportions of the walls seemed to become distorted as if we were in *Alice in Wonderland*, I finally said, "*Basta*," and swore that I'd protect us from that night forward. I bought three gross of white candles each academic year to keep us encircled in eighteen glass-enclosed lit votives, so that our uninvited guests, unable to cross the circle, were at least confined to rattling in the corners of the room. When the Taiji class changed venue and we were prohibited from lighting candles in the new space, I had half a box left.

It never fails to surprise me when small acts of personal devotion done for others come back to me as blessings in return; during the power outage, the thought of all those candles made my weary husband smile during his climb up seven flights of stairs in near darkness. Within a half hour, nearly two dozen lights were ablaze in our one-bedroom apartment: two in the bathroom, five in the kitchen, five in the bedroom, two in the hallway, four in the living room, and five in the dining room, keeping the darkness at bay and our spirits up. It was a Chanukah-like experience, but this Greek was inside the temple rejoicing, not outside howling in the dark.

DARKNESS, MOREOVER, IS NOT ALWAYS an enemy. It can be a loving teacher, even a friend—but only if steadied by patience, love, and courage. The first time I became aware of how that works was while I did the prep work for the Taiji class in that church. Having been given permission to come early to prepare the room (the church was too poor to have a custodian on a full-time basis), I swept the floor, arranged the chairs and tables, then burned incense, lit candles, and said prayers to keep the ghosts at bay. Not only did this ultimately train me to deal with fury, impatience, fatigue, and ego, it helped me to learn how to let go—to love what I didn't understand, make room for it in my life, and watch the results unfold.

First Presbyterian Church, Edgewater, NJ

Many times before class, I entered into a chaotic space chock full of chairs and tables strewn about for the church folks' needs. In addition there were books, papers, and partially consumed bottles of water lying haphazardly where they had last been used. I'd try to make sense of it, rearranging these objects—mindful that I was in someone else's quarters—as seemed best without being intrusive. Yet a sense of irritation would swell in me as I yanked things into some kind of order, furious that anyone would do such a thing to us—meaning *me*. My ego had raised its ugly head, and the absurd part was that, in a rage, I was clearing out a room for candles, incense, and Taiji.

Late one evening after class, I sat with a close friend on a bench beside the Hudson River, looking at the moon. A New York Harbor Police boat hurried by at a clip, and a minute or two later the strong wake it left lapped against the shore. It occurred to me, watching this in the utter calm that can descend upon you after practicing Taiji, that flailing about to clear a classroom in anger and impatience also left a wake, albeit invisible, and that its disturbance lingered much longer in the room than the boat's wake did in the water.

I began, thereafter, to hasten slowly, so the twice-weekly ritual evolved into a personal blessing as it slowed and steadied me, allowing me to shake off the irritations of the work day. Each step I took to clear the space physically and spiritually reverberated in me and in the building like a bell. However, as my mother would say in Greek, "This suitcase still has a long way to travel." Although I came to terms with how I prepared the Taiji space, I still had a long way to go in grasping how that affected my standing in the class.

Before each class began, Roy paused in the doorway to survey the space, sigh, and enter without further comment. He very much enjoyed intentionally ignoring my efforts. I never got a "good evening," never mind a "good job." If he bothered to speak at all it was to ask the same question—"Where's Barry?"—because he was always disappointed when my husband, the only other male in class besides him, didn't show up. He'd eventually drift into lotus position to begin our meditation, completely indifferent to me chafing and mumbling as I sat on my pillow.

The shifts were slow and subtle over the three years that I performed the rites. I calmed down and began, after more than a year, not to mind being ignored by *Sifu* (Chinese for "teacher"), because something unexpected became far more important: I had fallen in love with the church and, by default, accepted its other worldly occupants. Instead of offering prayers to protect us from the dead, to quiet them down and keep them at bay, I began to include them in blessing prayers that I read for the class and for *Sifu*. While I diligently swept the floor, I also chanted "Om," or combinations of Hebrew letters that reverberated through the church and me, and when

I had the time, I'd not only do the classroom floor but the one in the adjoining hallway as well. The mortar and dark stone that housed the space where we practiced became precious in their own right. I would sing out a greeting to the church when I entered to begin my preparations, and whisper good-night when I locked the front door after the class ended. It didn't matter if others were present; they were too focused on chatter to notice.

The work became its own reward; I loved and took care of the church and *knew* somehow, with absolute certainty, that it loved me back as much.

Usually I was the last, or among the last, to leave the building after class. Once in early spring, as my husband was pulling away in our car, I noticed a light in the church sanctuary, which was situated directly above our classroom. We were half a block away, but I couldn't in good conscience allow it to stay on all night, since the parish was struggling financially. I asked him to pull over and wait. I unlocked the red wooden door and fumbled in the dark, first into our classroom, hoping that with lights off I would be less likely to see one of the ghostly inhabitants. Although we had come to a peaceable understanding, I wasn't sure how I would react if I came face to face with one of them.

In one corner on the ground floor stood a turret,

which had become a storage closet that housed, among other things, an electrical panel that controlled numerous lights—but not the ones on the second floor, which meant I had to turn on a hall light in order to creep upstairs into the sanctuary, unknown territory, and search for it.

I did so, praying I was alone. I found the switch in an identical turret closet in the corner behind the last pew, and finally shut off the altar light. Making my way down the stairs and out the door, I was relieved that I'd had no unexpected encounters.

A few weeks later, we got the bad news that the church was being closed for good and put up for sale. We would have to find another space. The pastor, working late one night, stopped by the class and, while chatting with Roy, mentioned that part of the church had been built over an Indian burial ground, although the graves had at the time been relocated elsewhere.

The pastor knew that at least one ghost was rattling around her church, but she was completely at peace with it; she added that it had lately taken to switching on the light above the altar after it had been switched off. Recently, a parishioner had noticed this light was on and had been about to turn it off when a ghost appeared before her. Screaming, the woman had rushed out of the church, run home to call her mother in Korea, insisting she come to America to comfort her, and never returned to the church.

I realized that there but for the grace of God went I. The ghosts and I had, over the years, become friendly enough for them to spare me that drama. I was grateful, considering that, a few weeks previously, I had switched off the same light under the same circumstances. I suppose I had earned—having read all those psalms on their behalf and done all that straightening up—the right to be left in peace.

For the last month of our stay, all the classrooms became stockrooms for the customary stuff that a church accumulates in a hundred years and was now forced to sell off, so we were relocated upstairs to the sanctuary to practice Taiji. After class one Thursday, when I was performing energy work on Roy, who wasn't feeling well that night, I heard a *click* but gave it no thought, focused as I was on the healing. When we finished, Roy said, "I saw the ghost—a woman in a long striped dress from the 1860s, running across the opposite side of the room from the stairs to the closet." His finger traced her progress towards the now infamous closet in the back corner, which housed all the light switches. "Did you see her?"

"No. I was working on you."

Because I was in charge of turning on the lights in

preparation for class, no one else touched them, choosing to sit in the near dark rather than chance interfering with my rituals. As we prepared to leave that night, I returned to the closet Roy had seen the ghost enter. I am not a fan of overhead lighting, preferring the quieter illumination of wall sconces. As I turned them off, expecting to walk for thirty feet in dim light to the lit staircase that led to the front door, I found, to my surprise, that the center chandelier was on. Then I remembered hearing the *click* and realized the ghost had flipped on the switch to mark our co-existence. She had reached out in a gesture of friendship—showing me the way.

WISDOM

CHOKMAH IS THE SECOND *SEPHIRAH*, or sphere, in the Tree of Life. Simply put, it means "wisdom" in Hebrew. Moving from Kether—light that is closest to the Divine, and the initiation of faith—into Chokmah sets in motion the possibility of wisdom. Chokmah generates the earliest, most unformulated expression of consciousness, meaning the potential of all things possible. We, in turn, spend a lifetime sorting through these possibilities to find, and give definition to, our personal sense of wisdom.

Combining faith and wisdom in whatever we do is epitomized in the Tarot card the Fool, who is always depicted as not caring where he steps, having nothing to fear. In his own peculiar way, he knows that faith is driving his unconscious steps from moment to moment as he ambles along the precipice of life. Having done it all and survived—the very essence of how we learn to become wise—the Fool has chosen to get out of his own way and walk his talk.

Chokmah is represented by the color gray. The blinding white of Kether mixing with all other colors representing all possibilities, results in this very pale expression of humility. My husband, who speaks Yiddish, points out that a *chochem* (a noun derived from chokmah) means both "wise man" and, in slang, "wiseguy" or "wise-ass." It's not surprising that humility comes down to the distinction between a wise person and a wiseguy.

A wise person, like the Tarot's Fool, has nothing to prove, because the self is not in question. Humility is earned during a lifetime of making mistakes. Wisdom evolves when we realize how not to repeat them (because we usually do, in some form or another, until the lesson fully sinks in) and muster the courage to keep going till we get it right.

I am always amazed by the reluctance of those I consider wise to give their advice, even when asked. There's a slight hesitation as they consider what they think can be communicated, knowing that each person's experience is different enough that they must find their answer, always hard-earned, themselves. Often this reluctant advice is couched in a story, some similar situation that has happened to them. Their ability to discriminate, to discern the difference between what is eternally true and what is only "of the moment," is a real gift.

Oscar Wilde's definition of a cynic, "a person who knows the price of everything and the value of nothing," captures the essence of this distinction. So Chokmah at a basic level is the ability to differentiate between the knowing of a know-it-all and the true understanding that approaches wisdom.

I'VE TACKLED CHOKMAH a number of times, but the sephirah only started to make sense when I took a stab at concentrating on its aspect of humility for an entire year. Nothing was more humbling during that year than learning how the old adage "If you point one finger at someone, three are pointed back at you" is painfully true. Whenever I was upset by how someone had treated me and took a good long look at the behavior, sure enough there I was, doing the same thing to someone else.

The first time, to my horror, I realized this truth, I called Roy, who was very strict with me since I was serving by then as his apprentice in the healing arts. He expected more than I was sometimes willing to give. When he answered the phone, I confessed, terribly embarrassed, in a rushed tumble of words, "I took a good long look in the mirror, and I don't like what I see. You're right—I *am* a very small person who does big things."

He had leveled that accusation at me years before to underscore the frank truth that my instances of generosity were no more than acts of ego. That devastating remark had stayed like a burr in my side—and it hurt any time I recalled it. Because I was not ready to face myself, he had remained indifferent for the longest time to things I did for him, or for others.

My confession over the phone was met with silence for a good long minute. "It takes courage to admit that," he said at last, and cryptically added, "Let's see what we can do."

Several months later, he, who had for weeks been admiring a necklace of black tourmaline that I wore daily, received a similar one from me as an early Christmas present. Clearly, he liked it, because he wore it frequently. Four days before Christmas, during the last Taiji class of the year, however, as he floated onto his meditation mat and settled into lotus position, he draped a scarf around his knees and cleared his throat to speak. "Before I left home tonight, I was on a website where you can buy a beehive, a chicken, a goat, or even part of a cow in someone's name as a Christmas gift. This is a gift that can really help a person in need, and make an ongoing difference in their life. This is the true meaning of Christmas, not some... some stupid necklace." He was wearing my gift as he uttered those words and continued blithely on without so much as a glance at me.

A verbal slap in the face: I could feel myself getting angry to obliterate being hurt. My sheer inability to change the situation other than to acknowledge that I'd given the gift with the best of intentions, and that there was nothing to be done to remedy the situation, unexpectedly forced me to let go.

I thought, as I fidgeted on my meditation pillow, You've wasted a lot of time being angry in this class. Why not skip the usual fuming all night, exploding in anger, apologizing at 4 a.m. in an email, and behaving in a contrite fashion for days on end. Instead I chose to focus on the task at hand—studying Qi Gong and Taiji.

At the end of class, as I was turning off the heat, locking doors, and shutting lights, Roy came up to me and said, "I am so proud of you."

"For what?" I asked absentmindedly as I continued closing up shop. There had been nothing remarkable in my form that night. I didn't know what he was talking about.

"You didn't take the bait. You just let go of ego." He

gave me a big kiss on the cheek and added, "You get an A+ tonight."

I was speechless because it hadn't taken much effort at all to shift into something other than my habitual behavior, to not caring that I had been terribly wronged. This almost accidental act of being present and walking lightly on the earth was my first glimpse of wisdom. It also marked a change in our relationship. While Roy always remained my *sifu*, my teacher, he slowly grew more collegial in his exchanges with me from that time forward.

UNDERSTANDING

BINAH, THE THIRD *SEPHIRAH* in the Tree of Life, means "understanding" in Hebrew. The understanding of this sphere complements the wisdom of Chokmah; they support one another because one cannot exist without the other. Binah, however, like a strict mother, requires you to practice patience and discipline to fully comprehend a situation. It's an opportunity to learn how the bigger picture of life unfolds, and how, when these challenges are faced even with a modicum of appreciation, they have a way of opening up and resolving for the better. In other words, Binah demands maturity. For any upset in our daily lives, the response always involves making a decision, taking responsibility for it, and directing your efforts toward implementing it.

ALL OUR RELATIONS

I learned the hard way that spiritual trainings require facing oneself. The first one I attended, in Poland, was on Kabbalah. When I got to Warsaw, I discovered that my luggage had been mislaid on a connecting flight out of Amsterdam. After a three-hour drive to the hotel, I waited out an hour-long dispute over room assignments, sitting in the hallway until the other parties involved worked out their issues; eventually, I got a room, but had no clothes until the airline found the missing luggage a day later and someone from the airport traveled the three hours to the hotel to return it. Others kindly loaned me clothing in the meantime. It dawned on me then that the training had begun long before the lectures started, when the rug got pulled out from under me and forced me to free-fall.

Planning a trip to Brazil for my second training, in shamanic work, I, therefore, packed an extra set of clothing, underwear, and pajamas into my carry-on bag just in case my luggage got lost again. And to insure that nothing could go wrong, I arranged to get to Porto Alegre more than twenty-four hours in advance, so that—no matter what—I'd be there in plenty of time and not miss even one second of the program.

But I couldn't board my flight the Friday night my husband dropped me off at Kennedy Airport because I didn't have a visa. Although a travel agent had booked the flight, the person helping me was not the office expert in travel to South America, and because she didn't know, she hadn't told me that, at the time, Americans needed a visa to enter the country. My husband had forgotten his cell phone at home, so I had quite awhile to wait before he retrieved me that night. I had to take a deep breath as I sat in silence to consider my situation and relinquish any illusion that I was in control. Binah was quietly at work.

What were the gods, in playing this trick on me, trying to tell me? First, I considered whether the trip was meant to be, or was it some other training I was supposed to attend? Later that night, I emailed the teacher, Foster Perry, to tell him what had happened. He emailed right back to say that the same thing had happened to *him* once, and he urged me, as he had done, to go to the Brazilian consulate on Monday morning, get the required visa, and fly out Monday night. He would rearrange the training so that the most important stuff got delayed until I showed up. It didn't take long to decide I would go, even if it meant losing two full days with him. I emailed back that I would be there, but that, if he didn't mind my saying so, the entrance exams to his trainings were a bitch.

When I finally reached São Paulo, I found I had to wait four hours before boarding my connecting flight to Porto Alegre. Another flight was leaving two hours earlier than that from the city's second airport, but the woman at the information desk confided that São Paulo was infamous for its traffic jams, and that it would take two hours just to cross the city, let alone get to the airport. The clock was ticking, and I was slowing sinking into self-pity succeeded by a rising sense of anger at the world for conspiring against me.

Slumped in a chair in the main airport lobby, I looked glumly around me. After a while, I roused myself enough to realize I was wasting energy being miserable. Wasn't the trip meant to be a spiritual experience in which I could focus on change? Wasn't the habit of frustration, self-pity, and anger exactly what I wanted to rid myself of in life? So. . .what could I do this very moment, I asked myself, to break such automatic behavior? Reaching for my Bible, I sought comfort by reading a couple of psalms for joy, peace, and courage; my mood began to shift.

Somewhat fortified, I explored the airport and found the quietest and least trafficked location available to practice Taiji—right in front of the VIP lounge, from which not a soul exited and into which none entered. Nor did

UNDERSTANDING

anyone come within fifty feet of that deserted hallway where there were no shops. Facing a windowed wall overlooking a portion of the airfield, I stood silent, still, and breathing quietly for a few moments before starting the 108 steps of the form. I worked myself into the coils of energy that ran up, down, in, and out as I practiced.

At one point, while performing the third and final chapter, turning 180 degrees in the opposite direction from where I'd begun, I was startled to find Security—in the shape of a girl twenty years old at most, barely five feet in height—standing nearby and watching me intently. When our eyes met, she began to whisper frantically into her radio. It seemed that my behavior was being assessed as a possible threat, an off-medication moment, or both. I continued to practice and, as I faced her a second time, she turned her back to me to report her observations, lest I overhear what she was saying in Portuguese. I got it anyway through her body language, which needed no translation. This back-and-forth continued until I finished doing the third chapter a second time for good measure, wondering all the while whether I was going to be arrested for public display of Taoism. I gathered my belongings from the corner where I'd left them for safekeeping, smiled as I nodded toward her, and strolled off to get something to eat.

From that moment on, my luck changed. When I finished lunch in the cafeteria, I remained at the table, feeling a bit lost only because I couldn't figure out where to leave my empty tray. Some patrons returned theirs to the front counter, so I did the same. Apparently, such behavior was not common in the establishment, and, in order to encourage it, management was giving out free desserts to obliging customers. I ended my meal on an unexpectedly sweet note.

As they were growing up, my niece and nephew collected what I refer to as "airport pins"—though you can also find them in any cheap tourist shop in most cities—which have some kind of recognizable emblem of the city or nation where the shop is located. My brother, who triggered this collection craze, long ago advised me to enter any establishment I'd least likely want to in order to buy them.

The airport shop where I found the pins was empty except for me. Brazil, a rich and varied country, offered many emblematic choices, and I happily purchased several different ones for my nephew and niece, though they were outrageously priced; in return the owner liked me enough to give me a coupon redeemable at the airport chocolate shop for some free coffee.

Munching on chocolate and sipping coffee, I wan-

UNDERSTANDING

dered back into the crowded lobby and, luckily, found a seat. While people-watching, I noticed an ancient nun in a light gray habit doggedly pushing a luggage cart filled to the brim with her belongings. There wasn't a seat to be had anywhere. I called out and waved to catch her eye, and when I did, pantomimed offering her my seat. Overweight and tired, she lumbered over, pointing to the women's bathroom across a vast space where we stood. I nodded, and she left her possessions in my care. When she returned, speaking in Italian, she somehow made me understand that she'd just left Rome and was being reassigned. I, under no illusion that I could be mistaken for anything but an American, offered "Greca" as an explanation of my ancestry. She nodded her comprehension. Then I spoke the one Italian phrase I knew that only a Greek could or would say to an Italian, "*Una faccia, una razza*," meaning we two were of "one face, one race." She burst into laughter, and I joined her. She gave me her blessings by way of the sign of the cross, and slowly pushed onward to her next destination.

In an excellent mood, having decided I was right where I should be, I was ready for my own adventure.

MERCY

CHESED, WHICH FOLLOWS BINAH as the fourth sphere in the Tree, means "mercy" in Hebrew. Sometimes it is translated as "loving-kindness"—compassion expressed without strings attached, without judgment or expectation. Foster frequently says that compassion is the root of all real authority, and Kristos urges us not to forget to have compassion towards ourselves as well. This is an exquisite balancing act, and I began to learn it in my own way while prepping the Taiji classroom.

Twice a week I carried in a large leather bag filled to the brim with a box of incense, an incense holder, matches, eighteen ten-hour candles in glass votives packed into a wooden box to keep them safe, a Bible, and additional prayers I kept in a special notebook, as well as a meditation pillow, Taiji shoes, and the scarf I used to cover my knees while in seated meditation. The bag was heavy, but I carried it willingly to and from my apartment, in and out of my car, and up and down a flight of stairs to reach the front door of the church for our twice-weekly meeting.

Once in a while during the academic year, carrying the bag became unbearable when the routine (and mostly the heft of it) got to me. When that occurred, I stopped to consider the benefits gained by the entire class, and the joy the rituals and prayers gave me, and I managed to redefine the concept of "heavy" and shrug off the fatigue of dragging that bag around.

Only once in the three years I performed the routine could I not talk myself out of the funk. I called *Sifu* and asked, "Could this one night. . .could I please just be a beloved student like any other student in class, rather than because I've set up?"

"Of course." He understood that required him to get there early because I wouldn't.

I spent that prep time soaking in a hot bath. I was so relaxed I didn't want anything to interfere with it; I even chose a different route to get to the church, so no one could anticipate my arrival and expect me to do anything. I made it a point of not parking on the street until 7:30

p.m. on the dot, when the class was supposed to start. Hoping to tiptoe into the classroom with the seated meditation already in progress, I was climbing the steps when one of my classmates poked her head out the door and exclaimed, "Here's Eugenia—she'll know what's going on."

This does not bode well, I thought as I entered the hallway to find Roy in stunned silence, standing outside our classroom door, which was being occupied by a woman who taught tarantella and was talking a blue streak at him. As I drew closer, two classmates came down the stairs from the sanctuary and exclaimed, half embarrassed, "We were sitting in the dark waiting for you."

FROM TIME TO TIME, the tarantella teacher held her rehearsals at the church. She'd appear without warning and, if I left the just-cleaned and prepped room for even a minute, she would physically claim it. When I objected, she'd have some kind of convincing reason why she should be there (and I should go into another room and start prepping all over again). Hearing her dilemma, I sympathized and gave her what she wanted. But it happened every time she showed up, till one day it occurred to me that she always had a way to show her needs were more urgent than ours, and I even began to suspect that her stories were not perhaps completely true.

Outraged at being had, I responded to her plaintive requests from then on by slamming the classroom door on her mid-sentence. The last time I did that, my husband happened to have been in the room, watching the power struggle unfold. Not at all interested in the history behind my behavior, he'd sternly asked, "What was it that Jesus said?" Raising he arm above his head and pointing towards the church above us, he had continued, "In my Father's house, there are many mansions."

Oh, crap, I'd thought, *the yeshiva boy is quoting New Testament. Now I'm in trouble.* I'd grabbed the Bible, sat on my meditation pillow, and read psalms till Roy entered the room. Then I had raised the book in front of my face to hide behind it.

Roy had given me an uncustomary, "Hi, Eugenia," as he strode past me with a quizzical look on his face.

The opportunity to make up for my bad behavior came unexpectedly at a girlfriend's fiftieth birthday party. She had, unbeknownst to me, hired the tarantella instructor for her women-only celebration, to demonstrate and teach us how to do a dance dedicated to the Sacred Mother. I was making my way to her apartment, having parked in a guest spot in the garage, when the elevator door opened onto yet another level of the garage—and there was the tarantella lady in costume, anxious and confused. As soon as I realized that she was coming to my friend's party, I told her not worry about being lost, that I'd take her there, no problem.

A lot of mildly interested women, some of whom had had too much to drink, had by then created a less-than-optimal environment for teaching sacred dance. Since I believed that Taiji was a prayer in action, my view of the tarantella lady became much more empathetic and respectful as she did the best she could under the circumstances. I watched, paid attention, and learned.

Roy, however, unaccustomed to the unrelenting barrage in her story-telling because he relied on me to be the temple guard dog marking out our space, had simply nodded without uttering a word and walked away. The rest of the class, except for me, had followed him to the bottom of the stairs that led up to the church. (That night, there was no other space available.)

I faced her, shaking my head ruefully, and said, "You know damn well you wouldn't be in this room if I'd been here on time."

"Oh, but no, you see, we really needed to be here. One of the dancers is eighty-two years old, and she couldn't *possibly* go up so many steps."

"Never mind," I said, interrupting her. "This happened for a reason, to show me something. I don't know *what* just yet, but. . .thank you." I laid my hand on her shoulder, startled her into silence by giving her a kiss on the cheek, and did an about-face to find Roy still frozen in place at the bottom of the stairs with my classmates chattering around him like finches. With a sigh, I moved through the crowd and announced, "Follow me. I know where the light is."

I plowed up the stairs, wondering first, had I really just said I knew where the light was, and, second, which light I was actually referring to.

STRENGTH

GEBURAH FOLLOWS CHESED and is the fifth sphere in the Tree of Life. It means "strength" or "severity" in Hebrew and exactly expresses the tension between "allowing for" and "control over" war-like energies like fire and anger. The duality of respecting and controlling these forces is easily seen in the element of fire, which can illuminate our way, force us to change when a fire is "lit under our feet," or wipe the slate clean physically or emotionally so that we may begin anew.

Mention Geburah, and I involuntarily wince. The sphere is not unlike the Tarot card The Tower, in which lightning has struck, leaving the stone edifice in flames with people falling out of it. While I've made several attempts to understand this energy, it wasn't until I devoted a full year to it, during which friendships dissolved, four beloved friends died, doors in work situations slammed shut, and my car was totaled by someone who ran a stop sign and plowed right into me, that I got the essence of Geburah.

My clothes, fingers, arms, desk, and papers frequently gathered burn marks that year. My husband noticed after a few months, as I lit candles and incense in the morning hours for meditation and prayer, that my bathrobe was full of them and offered to replace it. I thanked him but grumbled, "No point, I still have six more months in Geburah and a year in Tifereth to follow—and it's all fire energy. You'd be wasting your money."

The losses that I experienced that year, as well as the physical burns to my person and my possessions, were sharp reminders for me to pay attention. I needed to take control of my life and not get swept away either in wasting energy by getting angry or in feeling sorry for myself. In other words, I had to mind my inner fire.

But I have never been a big fan of change, and I was *very* resistant to giving up what I had been comfortable with for so long. As a result, I was unwilling to fall asleep on many occasions during that period. Irrationally, I believed that if I stayed awake, I could postpone facing a new day and making new choices. Those lonely hours in

STRENGTH

the dead of night were marked by counting my losses over and over again, which of course was of no help to me whatsoever.

What I had yet to learn, on closer examination of The Tower card, is that even amid all that destruction and chaos, most of the structure remains intact, and that, way off in the distance, lies a clear path to a new direction in life.

There was no way for me to gingerly hoist myself up out of the rubble of loss and change. Not until I gave in to the sheer weight of those circumstances was I finally free of them and, therefore, able to take control of my life. Geburah forced me—psalm by psalm that I uttered daily, and word by word that I wrote weekly—to give way to detachment. The severity of Geburah, which I felt as loss, changed to a nothing-left-to-lose courage and strength required to make my way to a new life.

These days, even on an occasional sleepless night more often than not caused by the full moon, I no longer feel that I'm alone or that my prayers go unheard. This was made clear to me one year by a bit of Christmas magic.

A few days before December 25, the moon had been waxing towards full, but I could not sleep because one of my back molars was infected. I suspected it was going to have to be extracted the next day. Unwilling to wake up my husband, I slipped out of the bed and wandered into the living room to be kept company by our Christmas tree, adorned with treasured ornaments and twinkling white lights. I've always favored twinkling lights, and especially since I learned that, when combined with a live Christmas tree, they bring in the fairies.

It comforted me to know, as I lay on the couch with an ice-pack pressed against my jaw, that I had company while I watched one silly romantic movie after another on TV. I said a little prayer for the pain to ease so I could go to sleep. After awhile, I finally drifted off. My jaw relaxed into place, and the natural pressure of it released the infection from my gum, and with it the pain.

I woke up with a jolt to discover a bright light hovering not far from me.

The suddenness of my waking up gave the sprite a jolt as well—a globe of light about nine inches long, not unlike an old-fashioned Christmas ornament tapered into delicate points at the top and bottom and emitting a starlike bransel from its center. Within seconds, it had shrunk to a pinpoint of light, then vanished completely. Its tremendous brilliance, even as a pinpoint, gone so abruptly made it seem as if the entire neighborhood had just had a blackout. I ran to the window to discover the

STRENGTH

street lights and traffic light still working. I had, in fact, seen what it was not possible to see.

I lost the tooth the next day but retained a wonderful memory of what the impossible looks like, a talisman of how to mind my inner fire.

EVENTUALLY, I LET GO of the poor-me story I had lived with for so long and made peace with the only constant one can expect in life—change. One morning some months later, I awoke from a dream involving a modern interpretation of The Tower card, set in Fort Lee, New Jersey. I was walking up one of the main roads into town, which climbs the west side of the Palisades, goes through the center of Fort Lee, then descends on the eastern flank to the Hudson River. In my dream a huge glass tower was on fire. Along with some old acquaintances from the volunteer fire department in Edgewater, a neighboring town, we were trying to make our way through the traffic-jammed streets to put out the fire. It was slow going, and before we got there, I opened my eyes, dimly aware these individuals had long ago disappeared from my life—the recurrent theme of loss about to play out yet again. Still half-asleep, I considered momentarily whether to sink once again into sadness. Instead, an old Egyptian adage that Kristos once uttered came to mind: "If you don't like the story, don't tell it." Weary of reliving the same dreary plot line, I shifted my view from the immediate sense of loss to a bigger picture. I remembered my friends' unaware kindnesses during those years in helping me become less Greek and more American. Now fully awake, the story I told myself, and will continue to tell, is that I'm not particularly different from anyone else—people come and go in a lifetime. It's simply part of being alive.

The fires of Geburah fuel our intentions by teaching us to let go of what no longer serves us in order to make room for something better.

MIDDAY SUN

SOUTH ON THE MEDICINE WHEEL is, like Geburah, principally about intention. It too uses warmth, emotions, fire, and passion to promote growth and fuel our desires. On the Wheel the illumination (or inspiration) of East is "fired up" with the intention of South, where, as a late adolescent and young adult, you find the will to choose, and do, what you want in this life. Stating your intention, moreover, reflects achieving the necessary maturity to make a choice, take responsibility for it, and do whatever it takes to bring it to fruition.

One way I have learned to declare *my* intention and follow through is this: As soon as I open my eyes every morning, I say to myself, "Today is going to be a good day." Then I leap out of bed as a way of anticipating just that. This act positively shifts my mood, increasing the possibility that I'll be able to handle whatever comes my way. The ruse works better some days than it does others, but eventually, through practice, greeting the day joyfully not only determines how it begins but how it ends.

Legend has it that the Taiji moves arose from imitating animals. Watching Roy's interpretation of those wild creatures in the Taiji form was a sight to behold. None of us had any doubt, when he demonstrated Bear Walk, lunging from side to side as he swept his arms across his body, that he had *become* a foraging bear, or maybe one fighting another. Wiry in build and graceful in movement, his ability to execute Snake Creeps Down, his body skimming the floor with only a hair's breath of space separating him from it before he swooped upward into Rooster Stance, was beautiful to behold.

Snake Creeps Down

Rooster Stance

He urged us to find our own ways to express the essence of a bear as it walks, or the power of a crane as it stands spreading its wings. When the class practiced White Crane Spreads Its Wings, he would demonstrate how—in this overdeveloped region where we share our parks with geese—they'd pose to protect their territory if humans got too close for comfort. Not one of us failed to get it as, fired up by our imagination, we stood tall, occupying space fully to spread our wings wide with a don't-you-mess-with-me look in our eyes. And the closer we came to the animal quality of any move, the better we were able to master it and thereby intensify its healing effects on our body and spirit. (As I have said, Taiji, once solely a martial art, is now mostly practiced for increased longevity and health.)

White Crane Spreads Its Wings

MIDDAY SUN

At other times, Roy tasked us to do the form involving one of the four physical elements. How would we, he asked, perform if underwater, or emitting flames of fire? He challenged us to move through the 108 steps as if we were already masters of the form. In response, we imagined that we *were* masters and grew a bit taller, moving more surely with each step we practiced. Balancing the slower and fuller movements of being underwater with the more dynamic and freer ones of becoming fire, we did our best to extend our energy, our *qi*, to the tips of our fingers and beyond. He encouraged us to picture this *qi* touching the classroom walls and moving past them. All this mastery through mimicry was an organized exercise in setting intention.

REPETITION IS THE DIFFERENCE between success and failure, and because I'm pig-headed, I repeat my mistakes many times before I learn my lesson. Slowly, however, through daily practice of Taiji as well as reciting the psalms, my priorities have shifted and allowed for the accumulation of intellectual and emotional ah-ha! moments. But just as is physically true of mastering Taiji, changes in character never happen in a straight line or in rapid succession. It takes a number of seemingly scattered and haphazard incidents over time to eventually bring positive change to fruition.

During my early years studying Taiji, which coincided with my initial work in Kabbalah, I had yet to control speaking my mind and did so more often than I would care to recall or now consider wise to do. Once I shot off my mouth to Roy, advocating on behalf of other students about how he was running a class that I didn't usually attend. He lost his temper and refused to believe that I had been angry for any other reason than my own self-interest. While he would not throw me out of his classes for good, he refused to conduct any more private sessions with me. It was like that for quite a while.

At first I was hell-bent to prove I was right, so I turned to Psalm 7, which helps disprove all accusations against you but in return requires you to learn from your mistakes. The psalm has to be read twice a day for one week. A creature of habit—I did daily psalm work in the morning—I needed a reminder to read the psalm at night, and I hand-wrote it on an index card, so that I could leave it on my night table to read before I went to bed.

An hour later, I grabbed the card, reread the psalm, then ambled into the kitchen. Standing in front of the stove, I had to admit the obvious to myself—that Roy was entitled to do whatever he chose to in class. I felt badly about how I'd behaved. I touched the card to the gas flame, having already made my apologies to the angel connected with the psalm for burning a text representation of it. I set my intention to accept the consequences of my behavior and leave it at that. This freed me to apologize wholeheartedly to Roy and slowly begin to patch up the rift.

It was the first time I had ever deliberately chosen compassion over the need to be right, and it enabled me to begin to let go of childhood furies in order to become an adult.

Some weeks later, while preparing the Taiji classroom one very cold January night, I was lighting votives when—holding an unlit candle in my left hand and bringing it towards a lit match in the other, my left arm passed near but didn't touch either the glass container or the flame of an already lit candle. Nevertheless, a narrow line of fire, which looked like a gas flame with a blue base and an orange tip, spontaneously traveled from my wrist, the side of hand where my pinky is located, down my inner forearm to my elbow.

Oh, oh, I thought, *do something quick*. I blew out the match before letting go of it so I wouldn't risk burning down the church. But as my right hand swept over to put out the flame, the orange portion disappeared as if someone had lowered the setting on a gas burner, and by the time my hand reached my forearm, the flame had completely disappeared.

Startled, I figured I'd better find out what damage got done and turned on a desk lamp to examine my forearm. I found neither my cotton sweater or turtleneck, nor my skin, bore any burn marks at all. There was no smell in the air of something having burned either. I couldn't for the life of me imagine what had happened or why.

Much later Roy pointed out that the flame had taken the path of my heart meridian. I didn't have the courage to actually tell Roy this, but eventually I came to believe that flame had heralded my getting a bigger heart. And just maybe the angel for Psalm 7 had, in a private joke, signaled back that my prayer had been received and processed.

STILLNESS

Let's consider this enlarging of the heart, the spirit of generosity, in a wider context. If anyone had said to me that I would learn to love Nature by observing it from the back of a factory that stamped out metal buttons, in the middle of an industrial zone wedged in next to a highway and opposite a railroad track, I would have been surprised. But I did. Nature, I discovered after a number of years of observation in such an unlikely setting, is tenacious and in its tenacity graces those who bother to notice how it softens even the harshest of landscapes.

When I started working for a medical billing firm that rented office space on the second floor of that factory, I was disheartened, because the side of the building where the parking lot lay seemed such a desolate place. Along the boundary of the property ran a chain-link fence topped with rolled barbed wire. The other side of the fence, no better visually, was occupied by yet another factory, a dark, cavernous space where steel objects were manufactured to order. That building's open back lot had been rented to a construction company that stored oversized trucks outfitted with forklifts, buckets, and cranes of every type and size—the stuff of every toddler's dreams.

Lunch hour, nevertheless, became my classroom—not only to practice Taiji but, without realizing it, to learn the rhythm of the plants that would grow, thrive, and die in such terrain, as well as the rhythm of the animals that, over time, began to gather to watch me do the form. Eventually I learned that, when the seed heads of the wild grasses, tangled in the fence where I parked, grew purplish, fall was around the corner; and that, when twenty-eight doves chose to huddle in the pines outside my window in January, the midwinter thaw was not yet in sight.

Seven or eight trees grew on either side of the chain-link fence; in between there were a few bushes and flowering weeds in the summer. To the uneducated eye it seemed an unlikely place to practice the form, but I had an hour for lunch and didn't want to waste time traveling back and forth to one of the nearby parks. Besides, driving during lunchtime anywhere in Bergen County is hardly conducive to relaxation.

A rather large tribe of starlings was the first to take notice of my endeavor to be lighter than air. Someone in the factory always remembered to feed them scraps at lunchtime. They would pick through the offering, their black wings fluttering. When they were finished, they'd gather on a few branches of some taller tree on the lot, chatting. They ignored me as I walked to another large tree farther back on the property.

I began to practice, rarely finishing the 108 steps, either focusing on what I had just learned, or trying to correct some move because *Sifu* had pointed out it was not up to snuff. My unwritten rule when practicing Taiji, if I was clearly doing a move wrong, was to go back two moves to discover where the mistake had really begun. Whether it had to do with my posture—the position of my shoulders, elbows, or knees—or the swiveling of my hips, I'd spend weeks trying to get the flow of movement from one position to the next memorized until it took no effort to do it right. For the half hour or fifty minutes available to me, my arms, thighs, hips, and torso would go up and down, left and right, and back and forth over and over again till I felt comfortable with the move.

Noticing the silence one day after weeks of this routine, I looked up to find thirty pairs of starling eyes zeroed in on me as I seemed to dance in the wind, then stop, dance in the wind, then stop again. More than once I wondered what they made of my performance, having been told that starling males become quite acrobatic during mating season in order to attract a female. Nearly every workday, I'd do my dance, yet no human showed up to dance with me. Did they consider me hopelessly unable to attract a mate?

Regardless of how successful my practice session had been, when finished I always stood a bit taller, shoulders a bit straighter, and ambled catlike the four hundred feet back to the front door with thirty black heads tracking me in silence. They were like boys in the hood hanging out on the corner, watching me and life go by.

Slowly over time as the seasons unfolded, I became aware of beauty in that landscape where it was least expected. The trees, weeds, grasses, flowers, and bushes, as well as the birds, feral cats, and one brave rabbit that hid in the shadows, became dear friends who kept me company, bearing witness to a dance I did that was my contribution to the fleeting beauty that came and went there. In those many brief lunch hours, we became familiars. I hailed the wildlife and plants as I reached the spot under

STILLNESS

the biggest tree, touching as many of the plants as I could to say hello, and again to say good-bye when I headed back to the office, with thanks for keeping me company.

I had one wonderful moment when all kinds of birds gathered together in what looked like a great big block party. It was a warm fall day, and the five trees were fully turned in brilliant yellow and red. Among them, some yellow snapdragons, moss, and wild grasses were still holding out, gulping in the last of the warm Indian summer sun.

Starlings circled above me as I worked on my moves. Then suddenly they shifted into stillness, watching me do Taiji while they perched on the edge of the factory roof, having come to a temporary truce with the visiting wild parrots there to investigate the possibilities offered by this new territory. Suddenly there was a noise at the makeshift watering hole, where water from a heavy rain the night before had collected and overflowed into the worn ruts of the parking lot. The waterlogged area quickly filled with starlings, crows, parrots, finches, sparrows, even a few doves, chirping, squawking, and bathing while gulls floated serenely above us. None of them, during that riotous behavior, minded that I was only a few feet from them, repeating my moves. We were all celebrating the last of the summer sun in our own way.

As that practice session came to an end, three fearless parrots, which had perfectly camouflaged themselves in a bush five feet from me in order to observe the eddies of energy that collected and swirled as I moved through the form, burst forth when they'd seen enough, giving me—in spite of the racket going on not far away—a real start.

Eventually what I had once thought of as ugly became fully alive to me, a place where on rare occasion I'd get treated to the sight of a hunting eagle gliding by, or a hawk that smaller birds were chasing out of their nesting area. Since I was no longer a stranger, even the rabbit that hid under a crane lying on it side—to avoid the claws of bigger birds—would keep still only feet away while I did the form, albeit on the other side of the fence. From a comfortable distance, stray cats would also stop to watch me. The energy I created, in combination with the reciprocal good will generated in turn by the wildlife that gathered there, shifted the back lot so much so that even the two-legged creatures took notice.

The factory workers all kept watch, hidden behind their open doors and windows. When I went away on a trip for more than a week, two of my co-workers were asked what had happened to the lady who—at loss for words, the questioner swung his arms from side to side. Relieved to find out that I hadn't disappeared, just gone on vacation, from then on he (and others) hailed me coming to and from my practice, asking how well it had gone and how well I was. The exchange of pleasantries brightened everyone's day.

Once, construction workers from the other side of the fence, as they were pulling out a piece of machinery facing me not more than a yard or two away, asked what I was doing, followed by, "Does it work?"

"Yes," I replied. "When I'm finished, I feel like you would if you'd just stepped out of the shower and had a cup of coffee—refreshed, ready to start the day. I can face the afternoon's work much better." They nodded and, from then on, let me be. Gentlemen don't interrupt a lady showering in public, though on some non-verbal level they must have registered my joy because I did it almost daily, weather permitting. As long as the temperature didn't go above 93 or below 20 degrees Fahrenheit, I was out there practicing. When it snowed or rained, I'd do the form under a long awning that covered the first fifty parking spaces on my side of the fence.

Because of seniority and age, I was eventually offered the opportunity to park under that awning, a perk coveted because cars parked there were protected from the elements, and because it was closer to the front door. I thanked my supervisor but declined the space, explaining it meant I would no longer be near the tall grass and able to watch the sparrows feeding on the seeds each morning as I pulled in. She exclaimed in exasperation that *I* was a bird.

Probably she meant that I was *for* the birds, but to have become like them would for me have been an achievement. So like the younger staff with less seniority, I continued to park farther away. But they all noticed that, unlike theirs, my car didn't regularly get pelted with bird droppings. With some glee that just couldn't quite be kept under wraps, a co-worker once pointed out, "Look, finally your car got hit, too."

To which I replied, laughing, "It was an accident."

THE FACTORY RECEIVED DELIVERIES in the back of the building, not far from where I practiced. From time to time, drivers, nodding their thanks as I made way for the truck to come and go, would stop to ask what I was doing. One young driver brought me back full circle to Sifu. He stopped his truck and got out. As he approached me, he asked the usual questions, what I was doing and did it work. Then he asked, "Who's your teacher?"

"Roy Lucianna. He teaches Taiji in Edgewater."

He laughed, shaking his head. "No kidding! Roy is

teaching now! He used to work with my mother in publishing. She told me that he'd be out there at lunch time, rain or shine, practicing. So now he's teaching. My mother would come home, and all she'd talk about all night long was Roy said this and Roy did that."

I asked for his mother's name and got it, but she had passed away a couple of years earlier. The young man returned to his truck and took off. I finished my practice session and called Roy, who was not so terribly surprised by the six degrees of separation.

"I've been thinking about Joanne for a couple of days and considering whether or not to give her a call. So you spoke with Joey, huh? All Joanne would do all day long is talk about her son Joey this and her son Joey that."

I was grateful that Roy couldn't see or hear me laughing.

ALL OUR RELATIONS

MIDNIGHT SUN

TYPICALLY, IF YOU CHOOSE TO MOVE through the Medicine Wheel seasonally, beginning in the East with spring, then South with summer, you reach the West for autumn. But the midnight sun is North on the Medicine Wheel, and while Tifereth, which follows this chapter, is all about healing through the warmth and light of the sun, I wanted first to examine how I reached homeostasis by coming to terms with loss and death. I have therefore taken the four cardinal directions out of context here and jump forward to North.

The bulk of any spiritual work consists of having the courage to look at yourself in the mirror—usually an eye-opening endeavor. In some esoteric circles, people use a dark mirror to see what's hidden behind the facade that we're all are so good at presenting to the world.

I have been graced, however, with intervention from the departed and the living that has allowed me not only to take a good look at myself, but also to see death and dying as steps towards a new beginning. This is how Native Americans view the direction of North in the Medicine Wheel—the place of the midnight sun.

The North symbolizes winter, old age, death, and rebirth (the direction of East being dawn and childhood; South, noon and adulthood; and West, sunset and maturity). Old age, like the long nights of winter, is when we slow down and sift through our life experiences. As we approach our final years, we assess lessons learned, pass along our hard-earned wisdom, and prepare for the transition into and beyond death.

Having helped Roy die has meant coming to terms with dying, the afterlife, and asking myself some very difficult questions.

THE DAY HE WAS BURIED happened to be the one I began a weekend workshop in Bergen County with Foster and Kristos. By a bizarre coincidence, Roy's burial took place around the corner from where the workshop was being held. After the funeral I walked from the cemetery into the classroom, late. Kristos exclaimed, "Hi, Eugenia. Why are you all in black?" He knew, of course, but wanted to kid me into shifting my energy. Later that morning he asked, "What is the purpose of life? . . . Eugenia?"

I answered wearily, "The purpose of life is joy."

I was suddenly transported back to California, two months earlier, during a training with them where Kristos spent a number of days hammering in that point. The class was having lunch at the Malibu Country Mart, a small square with a park and playground, surrounded by shops and restaurants. The sounds of children laughing and playing drifted by and joined the murmur of adults enjoying one of those magnificent summer days in outdoor cafes along the coast. Looking around in disbelief, I had felt as if I was staring at a mirage.

Foster, sensing my disconnection, whispered, "It's all right. You're safe here."

Three days before arriving in California for that training, I had watched Roy hesitate to answer the question of an American Indian Shaman I'd asked to work with him: "Well, man, do you want to live or do you want to die?" Roy kept glancing at me, not sure what to say. I'd learned long ago that what a person says about wanting to live, and what the soul has decided on that very subject, can be in conflict. When the Shaman excused himself a few minutes later, I kneeled down before Roy, kissed his hand, and said, "If you want to go, go. You have done well by me."

It wasn't as if he, who had ended palliative chemotherapy, choosing quality over quantity of life, didn't know the final outcome—though he kept insisting to those who needed to hear it that he could still beat the cancer. But how comfortable was he with his choice?

When the Shaman returned and I excused myself to make them some tea, I heard Roy murmur something inaudible, to which the Shaman replied, "Okay, man, then I'll give you enough energy to get your affairs in order."

I was still hoping by some miracle that he would pull through. But overhearing that bit of conversation forced me to face my conflicting emotions and wishes. While I was working on Roy to help give him respite from constant pain, I was outwardly calm and helpful. But during those last months when I was not with him, I cried without fail at the loss of Taiji class, and the pending loss of him, every Monday and Thursday evening when the class would normally meet. I needed—once I had told him not to worry about me—to prepare to let my beloved teacher go.

Two months later, during that Bergen County weekend workshop, as I sat, stunned at the loss of Roy, listening to Foster's lecture, he abruptly interrupted it to talk briefly about death. He began by repeating what I'd heard him say before, that he loved death and always chose to spend a considerable amount of time there between lives. Foster described the "Other Side" as having several levels that you enter based on vibration, a place where everything is effortless and there are no mistakes because all is perfect.

"Level One," he began, "is when you reenter the light. Level Two is an orientation. You review your life with others, your spirit guides. You are your own judge. You analyze what is recorded, you review simple things, the good acts, everyone you helped.

"Level Three is the physical—forests, meadows, deserts, animals—where you can study nature. Level Four is the realm of creativity and the arts.

"Level Five is the level of research, knowledge, and study." Foster explained that not everyone gets that far. "This is a level where you *densify* your light. The more spiritual you are, the denser the light, and the higher the level you go.

"Level Six is where every known teacher and prophet has a school—hermetic, shamanic, Platonist, Pythagorean. On this level the light is at its strongest, where you see God and Mother God walking around.

"Level Seven is where you go back to light. It is a very dense level—Buddhahood, where the soul becomes a drop that goes back to the ocean."

At that point Foster resumed his lecture on the *sephirah* of Kether, the initial sphere on the Tree of Life, and I was cheered as I thought of Roy walking through a beautiful forest somewhere, maybe cracking a book or two and studying to his heart's content.

This reassuring image was furthered weeks later by a former Taiji classmate who occasionally did the Ouija board and was startled when my name came up. The message spelled out was, *Tell Eugenia that Roy is all right now.*

I MET WITH FOSTER AND KRISTOS again the next time they were in the New York area in late winter, about six months later. Before working on me energetically, Foster began to sing, the sounds he belted out otherworldly, a siren-like song washing over and through my body, drilling down into me at the DNA level and cleansing whatever negative energy remained in my body. Once he finished, and as he was preparing to work on me physically, he looked up to say, "Your teacher Roy is here sitting right next to you, wanting to participate in your healing. . .sound sometimes calls in the dead." He stopped a moment, cocked his head as if listening, and asked no one in particular, "Oh? You want to do the healing?" He yielded to Roy and sat back, uttering prayers under his breath while Roy, dead and gone for six months, worked on me as I had worked on him so many times the year before. That the veil dividing the living on Earth from the dead on the Other Side was truly gossamer began to condense into a reality for me from that day forward. When Roy finished, Foster continued his work on me.

A YEAR LATER, OVER A CUP OF COFFEE at breakfast with Barry, I announced that I needed to see a medium, something I don't normally do, in order to speak with Roy. Mystified, he asked why. I explained that I was finding myself carrying around other people's emotional pain, particularly those who felt an incompleteness over Roy's death, and needed to ask him how to release this pain that was not mine, that, otherwise, it was a situation guaranteed to eventually affect my health.

Barry remarked, "But Roy was *terrible* at letting go of other people's pain!"

"Exactly," I replied as if the point was self-evident, "and he's dead. With hindsight he must have *some* advice he can give me."

A week later I made my way to a medium I had heard give a talk at a friend's home. I trusted my friend's instincts to seek out this medium. As I sat down before her, she cautioned me that no one could predict who would come through. I nodded, said that I understood the limitation but knew full well Roy wouldn't miss the chance to talk, and, sure enough, the first thing she said on his behalf was something there was no way anyone could have guessed. Roy had made the remark to me years before when he initially got sick but kept the diagnosis a secret, and then repeated the exact words after I knew about his illness:

The cancer was not my karma. I carried it on behalf of someone I loved. When I heard this, I knew I was speaking with him. He continued, *I was happy to do so, even though at times, being human, I became afraid while dying.*

The medium continued to deliver his message as best as she could, and, as had been his custom on occasion in life to chastise me, he proceed to tell me, *You need to lighten up. Although you have inherited my mantle, I am still doing my work, but from this side.*

"Okay—" I was relieved to hear this and more than happy to let him deal with those grieving— "so what am I supposed to be doing?" The conversation was just like the talks we used to have, except he now was dead and a woman was listening to him and speaking on his behalf.

People go off their path, wander around, and eventually come back to it, and that's okay. Or they go off their path never to return to it, and that's okay, too. All of humanity is about to be elevated to a higher energetic level, except they have to go through a very narrow gate to get there. If they are carrying any attachments, even one, they will not be able to get through that gate. Sunday school, and the parable of the rich man going though the eye of the needle, crossed my mind. *Your job is to keep this narrow gate open for them, so they can pass through it.*

Wondering when exactly I had volunteered for such a task, I asked, "Great, so. . .what am I supposed to do? Call, email, write?"

You can do that, Eugenia, but in their hearts they know you are waiting for them.

Then he did a very Roy thing when it came to dealing with me and complained to the medium that he didn't know why I felt I had to come see her, since I hear him perfectly well.

I was most comforted to know that we were still keeping in touch, though I had no memory of it. I guessed we probably met during my dream life, and the results must coincide with the times I've awakened happy or at the very least really calm and certain.

As I watched Roy slipping away, there wasn't a whole lot of talk worth wasting energy on. One occasion, however, stands out during the short respite periods between energy sessions, when we sat on the back porch looking out over the ramshackle garden that hadn't been cared for in a while, and I ventured to initiate a conversation with him. It was a sunny afternoon in July, when small children from the nursery school down the block were shouting and laughing in the school playground; the steady voices of two housewives softly chatting also drifted by, along with the rasp of cicadas and birdsong. An occasional bark from a dog interrupted the general hum that overtook that afternoon. It's a working-class neighborhood with small yards butted up against each other into a crazy quilt of unremarkableness. But for that moment, with all of it bathed in sunlight and joyous sound, it really was the most beautiful sight I'd ever seen, and I remarked how his neighborhood, in its unawareness of itself, in being free of any sense of self-importance, was far more beautiful than many other towns in Bergen County I knew. He said not a word in return but grinned from ear to ear. I hadn't seen such a happy face on him in years, but he was clearly pleased that I had grasped an important principle of Tao—finding beauty in ordinary life.

AND I'VE DONE MY BEST day to day to remember just that. One way I've honored Roy is by continuing my study of Taiji. For seven and a half years, while I practiced with Roy, he'd often tried to get me to become softer in my execution of the form, by which he really was trying to get me softer as a person, something I never fully achieved while he was alive. My current teacher, Charlie Brenner, however, very often begins his corrections by complimenting me on the softness of my form (one of the four qualities—soft, round, integrated, and empty—of practicing Taiji). The joke has not been lost on me. After what I considered an appropriate amount of time of working together, I quietly answered, "Of course I'm soft. I've had to yield to death."

BEAUTY

TIFERETH MEANS "BEAUTY" in Hebrew, and at its crux it's about beauty through healing and healing through beauty. The color of this sixth sphere of the Tree of Life is sun yellow. And like the sun, which is central to the planets in our solar system, Tifereth is central to the Tree of Life, connecting directly to nearly all the other spheres. Therefore, it is also about being centered. Balance, beauty, light, and healing—like the chicken and the egg, it's hard to tell which comes first: Take anxiety, say, as an example of being imbalanced, which prevents us from being healthy or looking great.

When I entered my crone years, the years of wisdom, I celebrated the event at an eight-day training with Foster and Kristos in Los Angeles. (This became key for me to understanding the essence of Tifereth and balancing beauty and healing.) I was staying with friends, a couple very much in love, living in a home full of sunshine inside and out. There was a lemon tree not far from the front door, the only one in the neighborhood and the sole reminder that all of it had once been lemon and orange groves. In my effort to get my suitcase, winter coat, and gifts up to their front door, I hadn't noticed the huge lemons just waiting to be picked, because hardly any fruit was visible from the sidewalk. Neighbors were welcome to take what they needed whenever they wanted to. It's a home that evokes constant smiles.

As we sat around the table, drinking tea, I commented that Richard looked well and asked him how he was doing. Exchanging a look with Gail, he hesitated a moment before answering, "I just found out yesterday that I have prostate cancer."

It wasn't the answer I had expected. He was an old friend of Roy's who, during Roy's last months of life, had flown east to care for him and give respite to Roy's wife and his sister. Richard and I had grown close during Roy's final struggle with cancer.

I had learned from Roy that the first thing one does in such a situation is shut up, observe, and listen. And I did so that afternoon till Richard excused himself to take a call, whereupon I offered Gail the option of me staying

BEAUTY

with family farther away from the city. The last thing I wanted was to become a burden under their brand-new strain. "Nonsense," she replied. "We are so grateful that you're here."

I heard that refrain from either Richard, Gail, or both every day of my ten-day visit. I spent most of my time at the training, leaving around eight-thirty in the morning and returning after eight at night, but while I was in their home and in their presence I was supportive, energetic, and cheerful—not difficult to do because I believed he would have a positive outcome. Since Roy died, I had, more importantly, come to terms with facing illness and death. I could look back at the energy work I had done for Roy during the last months of his decline and realize the driven effort I had expended in "getting things done" had been my way of avoiding the reality, not only of his impending death, but of my own mortality, not to mention life without him there to hold my hand. And while I wouldn't have acted any differently, I would—could I do it over again—have spent my energy with greater ease, in essence have remained centered by letting go *into* the challenging beauty of watching someone slipping away from life, and therefore been of more help to him. In hindsight, I've come to understand why my husband so enjoys quoting Charles Maurice Talleyrand, France's great 18th-century statesman, who survived the

French Revolution. The advice he famously gave to his subordinates was "less zeal."

My practice of devotion carries me through difficult times. Reading the psalms in front of a lit candle, and burning incense, unfailingly bring me to an inner light and a way of feeling better no matter what is going on in my life. On our dinner break on the second day of class, a gorgeous, young, and very hip Londoner sat down next to me to ask me why I'd chosen to come to that training. When I explained to her that it was my fifty-eighth birthday present to myself, she exclaimed, "No, you're not fifty-eight!" She quickly added, "How do you do it?"

Embarrassed, I shrugged and said that I had lucked out. It was a combination of things—good genes, a quiet life, "But mostly it's the work," I said, pointing to Foster and Kristos. "Oh," I quickly added, "and lemon juice is very good for your skin, too."

But while looking good has been one beneficial dividend of cumulative daily work, it's been my practice that has kept me going strong and annealed my disappointments. So I was not surprised, in those early hours before sunrise, when I heard Richard quietly moving about in the kitchen. I joined him and listened to what he had to say. Sitting alone in the dark, he was, understandably,

BEAUTY

getting discouraged, wavering in his resolve. I reminded him that he was living in paradise, surrounded by sunshine and ever-present greenery, with the love of his life by his side. It was a life steeped in beauty and worth fighting for. I urged him, in order to deeply and completely heal, to focus on the present rather than on his regrets and past angers.

I loaned him my Bible and gave him a number of psalms that he could read, which helped him relax enough to return to bed and fall asleep. That prompted him to acquire his own Bible.

Two mornings later, over breakfast, I ventured to suggest that he might consider having an altar to face in order to say his prayers. There was a small glass table between the hallway and dining room with a beautiful blue mosaic cross hanging above it. It was the place where he and Gail charged their phones and upon which eddies of paper and stuff would gather in the currents of everyday life. They were both willing, and she asked, "Well, what should we put there?"

"How about that beautiful Buddha you have in the other room?" I suggested. When I returned from my training that evening, the space had been cleared away for Buddha, and, except for the phones that were still being charged there, the rest of the tabletop was empty.

Richard wasn't the only one whose courage wavered. In the glitter of Beverly Hills, where the training was taking place that warm and sunny spring week, and in the presence of two teachers who themselves shine physically, emotionally, and spiritually, I was being coaxed out of hiding in the shadows. For all my belief that things would go well for Richard, and in spite of my years of training having gotten me centered enough to help him during the quiet of deep night, what scared me to death was leaving behind the cover of being a student.

When Foster—aware of Richard's situation—informed me that I could no longer hide "like a mouse diving for some hole," I whimpered, terrified of letting go of the familiar. But he continued talking, laughing—welcoming me to Shamanism, where nothing is a coincidence. I could no longer behave as if I wasn't capable of doing the work; after all, he said, I had chosen that home and those friends to stay with at this particular moment. Richard had known and loved Roy, and now Richard, too, had cancer. "Nothing at this stage of the game in your training, or at your age," Foster went on, "is purely social or accidental." Reminding me to breathe as the realization that he was right sank in, he reassured me that I wasn't going to be doing my work alone. "You will, in fact, be the way-shower for your friend, to show him how

BEAUTY

to believe in spirit, even just a little bit, which is—after all—one of the purposes of living in this very materialistic world."

As I was having this conversation, I began to change how I viewed myself and recalled what I had already done for my friend by nudging him into considering choices to shape his *own* practice of devotion. The information had been readily available straight from my heart. I had had, when speaking to him, no fear, no confusion, no hesitation in communicating what I knew. . . .

That evening, I told Richard how the day had gone and how I now saw our personal challenges as intertwined. I needed to drop my habit of avoiding the spotlight, and he his habit of regret, in order for each of us to become whole. We shook hands, agreeing that we would prevent one another from retreating into familiar habits and begin moving towards the courage needed to break them.

A day or two after Buddha had been moved onto the altar, nothing else had been added or removed from the space. "Buddha looks kinda lonely," I observed, taking a sip of morning coffee.

Richard said, "Yeah, I was thinking the same thing. What do you think I should put there?"

"*You* need to decide what's important to *you*." After

a moment or two of silence, I added, "How about a candle and some incense that you could light while reading the psalms?"

By the time I was ready to return to New York, Buddha was flanked by a candle and an incense holder. As we stood there considering them, Richard gestured towards the additions and asked, "So what do they do?"

"Lighting the candle is an offering, a gift, and the incense sends your prayers upstairs."

He paused to consider this for a moment. "I guess we should find another place to charge the phones?"

"Mm. Probably a good idea."

VICTORY

THE QUALITIES OF NETZACH, the seventh sphere in the Tree of Life, come closest to those of the Native American Indian trickster, the overly amorous and unbelievably outrageous Coyote, who gets our attention by the silly or crafty things he does, mirroring back to us the foolishness of our own illusions. Netzach, which means "victory" in Hebrew, represents our victory in overcoming the illusion of glamor; but in Netzach, glamor is the shallow side of that deeper love embodied in the goddess Venus. As the planet Venus shines brightly even at dawn or dusk, so do the obstacles placed before us as we chase our dreams, bringing into clearer view the pitfalls that accompany them.

Not that the erotic (or the glamorous) are entirely negative aspects of love; after all, we've just left the sphere of Tifereth, where one heals through beauty and becomes beautiful through healing. However, if glamour or the erotic is left unchecked, one can descend into narcissism. And even if we avoid such excesses, who hasn't at one point or another uttered some version of, "If I only had X, then I could or would do Y"?

And although the following examples may be exaggerations—"If only I had a Mercedes, then women would go out with me," or "If only I were a size 4, then I would be admired," in this illusion-driven world, you need only to see a few car or fashion ads to comprehend how we are conditioned to believe more or less that either one of these statements seems true.

On a purely physical level, I dealt with this balancing act in my twenties, thirties, and forties, when for extended periods of time I frequented a gym. While I have never considered myself athletic, I was strong, diligent, and worked out pretty much at the same level of competence for years. But only when I was approaching a size 6 did those who preened in the ever-present mirrors available in gyms, mesmerized by their taut bodies, deign to made eye contact with me.

In my early forties, I worked with a trainer twice a week and went to the gym twice more to work out on my own. On days I didn't go to the gym, I hit the track and ran for five miles. One evening my trainer pointed out a good-looking brunette about my age who came to the gym every weeknight after work, as well as on the weekends, spending two to three hours a visit. She had the body of a sixteen-year-old: lithe, supple, stunning.

Several weeks later the brunette and I started chatting. One night, she confessed to me that she was terribly depressed. She was not ready to hear, so I didn't say, "Of course you're depressed—you spend most of your free time here. Just the thought of it depresses me."

Not long after that encounter, *I* realized that it was just as true an observation for *me*—having a fit, slim body was lovely, but it didn't make me happy either. Still, letting go of that pipedream didn't come easily—until I began to feel constant physical fatigue and consulted an MD-acupuncturist. She explained that I was far too *yang* in my physical activities and had to learn to become more *yin*. Once I achieved that, I could run a marathon if I wished.

Having to let go of pursuing beauty through physical activity in order to remain young-looking culminated in an *ah-ha!* moment that, while there is nothing wrong in looking and feeling great, there was something else that I couldn't yet define that was far *more* important—and my search for it led to an exploration of Kabbalah, Shamanism, and Taoism.

I didn't know it at the time, but that shift was Netzach elbowing me to redefine what feels right for me and having the courage to break through some common cultural assumptions.

By the time I reached my fifties, moreover, I realized that illusion isn't limited to the allure of the physical alone but appears in our emotional world as well. Here too, we can easily succumb to a need for others' approval. While a clear sense of right or wrong, for example, is crucial for every individual, you can't make the assumption that your personal definition of either is shared by others. You must be prepared to be comfortable with the decisions you make regardless of what others think. If you fail to do so, that is also a driving force of illusion. I am, for instance, sure there are those who thought that caring for Roy as I did during his decline was foolish. He was not family, merely my Taiji teacher. In the last year he was able to teach, as he became more and more ill and unable to fully function, I could have ended my relationship with him, as a few of his students did.

Roy, however, had allowed me to use him as a guinea pig to test out all the healing methodologies I had learned and wanted to practice. He gave me critical feedback on how to improve my efforts as well as a strong sense of

VICTORY

what I *was* capable of doing. As I worked on him through all his health situations, I was grateful for his patience and willingness to let me refine my techniques.

When I confessed to Foster that having worked on Roy in the last months of his life had placed me in an awkward position with some of my classmates, most of whom had no access to him by then and, therefore, no way of saying good-bye face to face, he startled me by replying, "Healers have a way of getting under the radar when people are ill." It was the first time he had referred to me as a healer.

A MONTH BEFORE I FOUND OUT Roy had stage-four lung cancer, he asked me, as he occasionally did, to do some energy work on him after class. For the first time, however, I could tell that whatever energy I let run through me into him was being blocked as if by a lead door, no matter how I tried to find a way around it. It was on the tip of my tongue to joke, What's the matter, you have cancer or something? but that wasn't a very funny joke, so I kept my mouth shut. I chose instead another tactic as we packed up to leave, hoisting on the several layers of outer clothing that December night required. I grabbed the black bags that he no longer had the strength to carry to his car, took a breath, and plunged in: "I've noticed lately you like. . .like you want to die?"

Not meeting my gaze, he answered, "I did, but I don't anymore."

Unconvinced, I continued, "Well. . .you seem really depressed."

"A little bit." By then he was running out of the classroom trying to avoid the conversation.

As I shut the lights and locked the classroom door, he made a beeline down the stairs and out the front door, trying to disappear into the night. I yelled at his back, "Not a little bit depressed, a lot depressed—like you-want-to-die depressed." I caught up with him as he stood by his car, and laid his stuff on the ground with a sigh. He was trapped—he couldn't leave until I lifted his bags into the back seat of the old Volvo station wagon. "Look, I've given this some thought. If you want to go, I will back you every step of the way, and help you."

He looked at me, tears in his eyes, and said, "You have no idea how much that means to me."

WHEN HE ENDED CHEMOTHERAPY about three months later, he allowed me to keep my promise. Had I not in fact become a small generator of energy to help him over the major bumps, most likely, like the majority of students, I would not have seen him either. And when the hands-on work I did for two hours at a time, which had for a while allowed him to drift off into peaceful sleep, barely gave him twenty minutes of relief before I had to start again, I went into a tailspin. The day that first happened, I came home wanting only to get into a hot bath of sea salt and baking soda. But the cat had peed outside the litter box, and getting to the cleaning products meant other stuff fell out of the linen closet, and nothing would easily go back into place. I whined to Barry that everything was falling apart.

He looked over the edge of a book he was reading and replied rather evenly, "Yes, everything is falling apart. Roy is dying. And you will pull yourself together and go back and help him as best you can for as long as you can, because it's Roy."

Stunned into silence, when I finally eased into the bathtub, I began to question my motives. Was I doing the work for Roy's sake, or mine? Was I doing it to make *me* feel good, or him? Finally I got it and grumbled as I soaked in the tub, staring at the ceiling, that he was going to be teaching me about my craft and about myself to the very end. Roy was showing me that surrendering to death is part of the work too, even as he himself struggled with it.

My illusion of doing something, anything, to counter

the inevitability of death gave way. I witnessed him little by little relinquish his roles as Pan, teacher, even fool—like Coyote, Roy was always ready to poke fun at the conventional platitudes that underlie all illusion—and slowly release his hold on life.

Having made the choice to help him during his decline was a fortuitous one that led to my eyes and heart opening to a new understanding that life and death are a continuum. I was given the opportunity, in return, to learn to believe in the unexplainable, to define what is important to me no matter what others think, and to grasp that the duality between life and death, between right and wrong, between reality and illusion, doesn't exist.

Freedom from that expenditure of energy, which at best is a revolving door with no exit in sight, has meant being able to turn my attention towards being creative as an act of self-love liberated from self-doubt. With nothing left to lose, this kind of love can take flight in any given direction. Only when I learned the lessons of Netzach was I able to start writing this book.

GLORY

Foster and Kristos once asked me to describe the symbol of Hod, the eighth sphere in the Tree of Life. I couldn't recall it, aside from the color being orange. They shook their heads in disappointment, saying it was a principle that I had to learn in order to teach. "The symbol for Hod is an empty orange circle with an orange dot in the middle," Foster told me. "You are the dot, dead center in your world—and Hod is about your ability to command it."

If Netzach is about dealing with illusion, Hod, which means "glory" in Hebrew, is its opposite. Hod requires pure mind with no emotions involved. It's about *logos*, the Greek word meaning reason and discussion, but it's also Greek for "word," so written or spoken communication is a big component of Hod, making it closely connected with the planet Mercury—named after the swift-footed messenger of the Roman gods—whose close proximity to the sun reflects its rapid orbit around it. Hod and Mercury, then, are both about communication and speed, and the link between speed and the word is *focus*.

Kabbalah is the written, spoken, and felt word. Words (and actions) can travel for a very long distance over time and space, by which I mean we can hold onto a memory of what has been said or done for a minute or for a lifetime. Furthermore, any long-lasting memory—good, bad, or indifferent—can positively or negatively influence how we interact with others.

The capacity to focus by asking the question, "Why do I do what I do in this situation?" permits us to choose whether to let go of a memory completely or not. How we arrange our memories in order of importance (how they line up on our empty orange circle, while we remain in its center) is therefore a matter of personal choice entirely in our control. The discipline of Hod in removing emotions from a given situation leads to mastery, the act of deciding what you want and focusing your efforts to get it.

The next question is, what do we focus *on*? Mercury, in the form of quicksilver, is used to attract and gather up gold (as well as silver) dust. So Hod is about attract-

GLORY

ing the authentic gold in us, which is truth. In Hod we can (since mercury composes the reflective backing of mirrors) also take a good look at ourselves and choose to reshape our thinking and behavior to develop a personal definition of what is true for us.

The Seventy-two Names of Virtue, part of the mental plane of Hod, can help. These are also referred to as the Seventy-two Angels of the Mercury Plane that we can call upon to achieve the highest forms of virtue. These Names are each composed of a set of three Hebrew letters that, when invoked, act to change a particular circumstance in our life. The first, Vav Hey Vav, for example, is used to awaken remorse in the heart for prior misdeeds. (I find it an interesting choice to *head* the list, since there is no way you can change for the better until you take responsibility for your mistakes. Otherwise, you repeat them.)

Examining the individual letters will further expand upon the idea of remorse and change. Vav in Hebrew translates to the letter "u" in English. All Hebrew letters also have a sacred quality that corresponds to a specific vibration numerically, spiritually, and physically. In this instance, Vav has the capacity to slowly correct karma. Double Vav has the quality of union with cosmic consciousness, and the letter Hey, equivalent to the English "h", is the letter of mastery. So the letters Vav Hey Vav, when placed together in this sequence, mean focusing on one's karma and changing it by mastering it, thereby becoming one with the universe.

This suggests that shifts caused by *any* of the Seventy-two Names of Virtue actually occur, not in the world around us, but deep within ourselves. They are one way to focus intention. There are others.

ONE OF MY FAVORITE EXAMPLES of this mechanism at work involves my first car, an old wreck of a green Datsun B210 I bought for five hundred dollars that looked awful but ran well. I was coming out of New York City one Friday afternoon in August. So was everyone else, and I got stuck in bumper-to-bumper traffic going up the West Side Highway for quite a while.

I noticed the temperature gauge moving closer and closer to the red. I exhaled, turned on the heat full force to cool the engine, rolled down the windows, and endured the sweaty trip as I inched towards the George Washington Bridge. I was unusually calm, utterly aware there wasn't much else I could do.

Just as I got onto the bridge, the needle crossed over to the red portion of the gauge. Well, I thought, it's going to take a miracle for me to get across. I was willing to accept whatever came next.

At that moment a hail storm began—solely on the GWB. I couldn't believe my eyes. Dime-sized hail kept pelting the car from one end of the bridge to the other, bringing the needle way back down into the black. Once I got to the New Jersey side, the thoughtfully timed miracle ended as abruptly as it began, and I was home safely in five minutes. No one I told believed it had happened—and to a certain extent, even having witnessed it, neither did I.

That is to say, inasmuch as from time to time I remember the story with a smile, sometimes I forget the point of it. To notice the small miracles that happen around you requires a conscious break in habit—and for me this has been about holding onto the feeling of isolation. While I'm not suggesting that I don't have to do my end of the work needed to reach a particular goal, I also must remember that someone always has my back—just for the asking; as long as I can stand still and relax in the center of my circle, I am then, if nothing else, at least in control of myself. Lao Tsu, in the *Tao Te Ching*, repeatedly makes reference to doing nothing in order to achieve something of lasting permanence—and slyly suggests, sometimes in half-jest, that in doing nothing there is hidden wisdom.

How, in the end, do these four aspects of Hod—standing still (doing nothing), speed, communication, and truth—fit together like the pieces of a jigsaw puzzle? Kristos once asked, "What is faster than the speed of light?" When no one replied, he answered, "Thought. Thoughts move faster than the speed of light." And thoughts are possible only with focus, which holds all four aspects in balance.

My ability to find connections in the Psalms, Taiji, and the Medicine Wheel, which reflects Mercury's ability to fuse together with other metals, mostly happens when I shut out the world to light a candle and incense, and then take a breath. It gives me the opportunity to slow my mind and allow it to drift across familiar ideas before I eventually bump up against some surprising commonality that not only sharpens each but very clearly highlights their mutual affinity.

Writing is a similar process. Facing a blank page means consciously choosing stillness as I sit at my desk and wait to begin, having faith that words *will* eventually come.

When I think about Hod and writing, I can't help but think as well about the Tarot's Magician, who stands before his tools, which lie on an altar as he raises a wand towards heaven. He is the master of his fate, expert in the use of those instruments, and therefore sure of himself—he has earned the right to wield them at will, centered in his circle.

To a certain extent, letting go, being certain that all will be well regardless, is not unlike staring at a blank page, knowing that all I have to do is jump off the diving board and begin. Most of the time I have no idea what I will write or where the words will lead me. Faith in the process carries me forward long before I can say with any certainty, after many drafts, that this is what I know.

FOUNDATION

YESOD IS THE NINTH SPHERE in the Tree of Life, and the moon is very much its symbol. Yesod is Hebrew for "the foundation," and Kabbalistically speaking, it's the sphere where self-reflection, intuition, and magic produce true independence—the very opposite of Hod, which is all about mind.

In its waxing and waning, the moon teaches that there is a rhythm to life in which change is inevitable. If you accept the lesson, then you have a shot at becoming fearless when facing the ever-shifting circumstances of life. Otherwise, the moon's mutability, and more to the point ours, lie uneasy in our hearts and minds.

It takes courage to look at one's reflection and own it. Think of the Snow White fairy tale: The Queen one day asks the mirror on the wall who is the fairest of them all—only to find to her horror she is slowly being eclipsed by a girl growing into womanhood.

Vanity aside, though, accountability marks the beginning of all independence. Therefore, accepting responsibility for mistakes, for being the architects of our lives, even for the reality of getting older, means taking ownership of our fate. Whether the moon is full, or dark, or somewhere in between, the amount of sunlight it reflects affects us as deeply as it does the tides—owning up to our feelings is our challenge, however much we'd rather blame the moon or others for our mood swings and, by extension, our troubles.

I can't think of "this lunar beauty" without considering the many evenings I've spent on benches along the river walk on the New Jersey side of the Hudson River. As the seasons roll by I've watched everything from ice float downriver in late winter to a welcome breeze barely make a dent in the heat of midsummer, and waited, sometimes with my husband and other times with a girl friend, for the moon to arc over Manhattan, clearing the city's skyline of glittering lights. We sit with cups of coffee or ice cream, discussing some triumph, disappointment, or heartbreak we've been mulling over, or some observation we've recently made. But always at some point during the conversation a respectful silence prevails as the moon more and more dominates the night sky, fully capable of competing with New York City lights.

The moon and the river have both almost imperceptibly worked their magic, lulling me into different sensibilities in which my concerns big and small have taken a back seat to simply being present. Now I no longer come to the moon and the river in order to seek peace; instead, despite whatever is going on in my life, I find I *am* at peace, simply happy to be out in the world with people I love. The concerns that I once agonized over have eased, and I'm not in such a hurry to replace them with others.

Perhaps we see more clearly in the dark because our intuition kicks in, or perhaps because nothing appears straightforward in the shadows. One evening, when I was in Palma de Mallorca for training in Kabbalah and the moon was just a day or two past full, I drifted through an outdoor hotel restaurant that was cantilevered over a hill to get to an almost empty walkway that looked over a stretch of the bay. I needed to shake off the news I'd just received in an email, regarding an older Taiji classmate whose sister, at age eighty and living in Johannesburg, had just been raped and was now on a anti-HIV regimen. I had spent some time in prayer for the sister and needed some quiet to get over the inexplicable violence of the news. As I neared the end of the dark walkway, in one corner a couple was embracing in a passionate kiss. The man saw me approach and tilted his head back to let out a staccato yelp, almost as if to warn me off. I stopped, recognizing the technique as one Roy taught to try to bring *qi* up from the depth of our lower *dantien* (the area of body that is two inches below the navel and about the same distance behind it) in order to stop the world with our voices.

I wasn't going to be put off so easily, especially when the walkway could have accommodated fifty people, much less three, without issue; I strolled over to the railing as far from them as I could to contemplate the water, the moon, and moored yachts off in the distance.

A few moments later the pretty young blonde, about fifteen years the man's junior, detached herself from his grasp and approached me in a unsteady gait to ask me for a light. As it happened, I had matches with me, fished them out of my bag, and handed them to her. Once she lit her cigarette, she asked me what had brought me to Mallorca, and I told her. As we conversed quietly in the dark, the man uttered another staccato yelp, to which she responded by hurrying back to him.

I had had enough of the would-be Tarzan and turned towards the hotel. With a shiver it occurred to me, call it intuition, that the young woman was tempting the fates, because this man seemed capable of great violence. An image of him beating her surfaced in my consciousness, and I tried to shake it off with a couple of deep breaths. Eventually the lovers caught up with me, and as they walked by she called out a breezy good-night in my direction. I answered, "Take care of yourself." Her head snapped back to give me a startled look as he grabbed her hand and dragged her off down the street and into the night.

That exchange was intuitive, but there is also magic, an aspect of Yesod, that doesn't have to be about the fantastic. When some moment in our life fuses together stillness, intuition, and intent, everything falls into place without any effort at all. The magic happens almost accidentally. We've all experienced this—a chance meeting in the supermarket with some talkative soul who is preventing us from going further down the daily to-do list. But having acquiesced to the moment and chosen to listen to what was being said, even out of mere politeness, we end up stumbling onto a solution to some problem we've been baffled by for some time. Or we find out in hindsight that the unwanted delay kept us out of the car long enough to avoid an accident at an intersection we could have been involved in had we been there a few minutes earlier. It's always the unexpected and surprising that startle us out of sleep-walking through life and interrupt the habitual views we have of ourselves.

I once complained to Roy that I couldn't still my mind enough to meditate. Having tried and tried, I'd become so frustrated I'd given up, deciding it was something I'd never be able to do. No matter what, even with the best of intentions, it wasn't long before I became distracted and, as many times as I could refocus, there were equally as many when my mind would wander. Since he and I had been talking for a good half hour before I brought the issue up, I had already settled down in his presence. He suggested that we do a partially guided meditation together. As we sat facing each other in half-lotus position, he instructed me to breathe quietly for a while, then imagine a thick mist descending around me and, when it lifted, see where it had taken me.

I saw myself as a man riding a dark brown horse somewhere on a immense plateau surrounded by distant mountains, some high enough to be snowcapped. My horse came to a halt as I approached my home, a tent. It had just finished dawning, and the valley, still cold, was filled with early morning light. Entering my home, I sat down to eat with my wife, children, and parents. The space was ringing with laughter.

Then, unexpectedly, a mist descended once more, and

when it lifted, it was once again daybreak in the same landscape, and I was on my horse and approaching a Buddhist monastery. My entire family was inexplicably dead. Having lost everyone I loved and with nothing to live for, I resigned myself to becoming a monk. I dismounted from my horse, picked up a rock, banged three times on the monastery door, and waited. Impatiently, I again banged three times and tossed the stone away in frustration, but continued to wait for someone to open the door. This vision was so unexpectedly real, my eyes flew open, and it ended.

I described to Roy what I had seen. He commented on the beauty of the images and their symmetry, hesitated a moment, then asked, "Was I there?" I scanned the faces of the family and shook my head. No one among them had reminded me of the essence of Roy. Then I recalled the final image and smiled. "Of course. You were the monk on the other side of the door about to let me in. Some things never change."

THE MEDITATION SHOWED ME clearly enough that the frustration I had experienced trying to meditate was mirrored in the frustration I, as a bereft man, felt waiting for a locked door to be opened. And in some sense the two situations are one and the same. I needed to own up to the fact that I alone was responsible for not practicing often enough to overcome my habits. Simply waiting for someone else to open a door that only I, with practice and patience, could open for myself was not an option. So Yesod sets us magically on our path, showing us where and how to build our own foundation.

KINGDOM

Malkuth, Hebrew for "the kingdom," is the tenth sphere in the Tree of Life, and the culmination of the previous nine, so it's the densest of them all. It is where our egos are the strongest and our life challenges (karma) emerge on a physical plane. We need, in response, to keep our egos in check in order to achieve harmony. We face resistances deep within our subconscious, and we overcome them by developing the will power and discipline to reshape our character, and thereby our fortune, for the better.

For me this challenge was expressed in the first three years I studied the Taiji form. They eventually led to understanding the difference between excelling at the form in an academic way and attempting to become a living embodiment of the Taiji symbol. I had to let go of any expectations, my never-ending need to master the form at breakneck speed in order to feel I was worthy of notice.

After I attended my first three classes, Roy asked if I practiced yoga, dance, or some martial art because I could see how a move was executed and almost immediately mirror it. No, I practiced none of them, and couldn't initially see what the big deal was. When I did see, pride—at the ease of my ability—set in.

Having spotted this bottomless desire to keep outdoing myself, Roy chose to slow me down to the rest of the class's tempo rather than indulge my avarice. He remained indifferent to my impatience, frustration, and anger, which frequently reared their ugly heads. I kept asking myself, "Haven't I practiced at home, attended more than one class a week, paid attention and worked diligently while in class? Why shouldn't I be rewarded with perfecting the form as soon as possible?"

This insatiable grasping caused me to suffer, because Malkuth, the sphere of all things physical, and most certainly of ego, can be thought of as hell on Earth. Not so surprisingly, then, Taiji class became a hell of my own making, particularly because, during those lean years, I watched less capable students get more of Roy's attention and, as a result, receive praise for their endeavors while I was ignored. All I could count on in class, each time he passed me by, was the inevitable rumble he made as he cleared his throat and walked on.

Once I caught on to this routine, I complained to friends in class. They, too, had noticed it. When I returned from a two-week trip, two of them excitedly came up to me and said, "Roy paid you a compliment while you were gone."

At last! I thought, and eagerly asked, "What did he say?"

"That no one prepares the room as well as you do." It wasn't what I wanted to hear. Gradually I gave up on praise and waited, at the very least, to be corrected in the form. But he continued to say very little to me.

It took years to let go of being less than gracious while watching him teach the same steps to the same students over and over again without what seemed to me any measurable improvement. Finally, I complained to him in private about how he never gave me any corrections.

He looked down for a while and then his eyes met mine, disappointment in his voice as he explained that his teacher had ignored him too for years, until he started to get better and better at the form, and then the corrections began to come week after week.

Though I felt ashamed about complaining *and* about

being scolded, I somehow managed to hold my tongue over the lack of correlation between his experience and mine. Roy, by his own admission, had initially been rather clumsy at the form. While his teacher had rewarded him for working hard and practicing till he did the form well, I was not getting the same treatment for the same effort.

Eventually I began to understand that he chose to teach those students who struggled the most first and foremost (whether they had less aptitude or less discipline didn't matter), and to teach them well, because it was the only way he believed it was possible to demonstrate his integrity as a teacher.

I had failed to grasp, however, that my classmates *were* improving on a level that went deeper than simply executing moves in Taiji. All of us, after years of practice, had shifted in our fundamental grounding upon this Earth. Once, while we were standing, about to begin Qi Gong exercises, Roy stunned us with an unexpected compliment: "You have all become very capable and strong women. Sometimes it's intimidating to stand here and face you."

I wish I could write that I changed in some magical flash of enlightenment; it was, instead, my sheer exhaustion at bucking his system for so long that finally led me to not care one way or another. Gradually, with hindsight, I came to see I was being taught patience in order to sand the sharp corners off my ego, which would ultimately allow me to do the form better. *That* was my salvation. My teacher had simply waited me out.

Only when praise or correction meant nothing to me did I become lighter, happier, and surprisingly better at the form. By patiently standing by and listening to how the other students were being taught, I learned not to push the river. It slowly dawned on me that studying the form had very little to do with clearly measured outcomes consistently strung together week to week like pearls on a string. Studying the form went beyond executing 108 steps rapidly and with ease. It meant being able to feel the joy in gathering stillness within before even taking the first step.

Finally, I came to prefer watching how my teacher coaxed the best out of fellow students, content to wait, or be called upon to be used as an example of the martial arts application of a move, knowing my trust in *Sifu*, and my ability in the form, would keep us both safe in the endeavor.

When I no longer cared to be quick or clever at the form and had stopped complaining about how, when, and what I was being taught—thereby giving my teacher the respect he deserved, and finally learning to care about, and pay attention to, the progress of others—only then did he single me out as an advanced student to whom, on rare occasions, he gave advanced student corrections. And this led me to helping teach beginners in Roy's class.

SETTING SUN

THE DIRECTION OF WEST on the Medicine Wheel is harvest time—reaping what you've sown and offering thanks. This is not unlike Malkuth, where everything achieved (or not) in the previous nine spheres comes to fruition. With any luck and a great deal of fortitude, we've stumbled through life's difficulties to develop the strengths to survive and even thrive under challenging circumstances. We arrive at a place where human frailties, ours as well as others', show us that we are all in the same boat, deepening our capacity for compassion.

The West, therefore, is about maturity. Having learned what no longer works for us, we let go of it completely. Writing this book has been *my* way of relinquishing what no longer serves me. Who I was when I began my personal search for happiness is not who I am now. Life experience alone is, of course, enough to change anyone. But I began my spiritual endeavors with the express intention of becoming a better daughter, sister, aunt, stepmother, wife, student, and friend. Am I? I have trained myself to use tools to reflect upon those aspects of my personality that don't do me or anyone else much good—impatience, judgment, anger, and most of all pride—and made it my business to work on them. While being mortal means that nothing is ever a hundred percent, I've done my best to reflect upon and adjust my behavior, so I'll do better next time.

The journey around the Medicine Wheel always returns to the initial step you have to take on any quest to achieve a goal—having faith. Combined with diligence, courage, and self-awareness, faith brings us closer to that goal through devotion to something greater than ourselves. Along the way we acquire the ability to instinctively know that we have been placed on this Earth to love and be joyous regardless of what or whom we encounter.

I recall with great fondness what Roy told me early in my training, which I didn't much appreciate hearing because I was well aware that I couldn't yet do it: "Eugenia, as you get your shit together, you will attract